TIFFANY'S

20th Century

A PORTRAIT OF AMERICAN STYLE

TIFFANY'S
20TH CENTURY

A PORTRAIT OF
AMERICAN STYLE

BY JOHN LORING

HARRY N. ABRAMS, INC., PUBLISHERS

Editor: Margaret Rennolds Chace
Designer: Carol Robson

Library of Congress Cataloging-in-Publication Data

Loring, John.
    Tiffany's 20th century : a portrait of American style / by John Loring.
        p. cm.
    ISBN 0-8109-3887-1
    1. Tiffany and Company. 2. Decorative arts—United States—History—
20th century. I. Title.
NK7398.T5L66 1997
745'.0973—dc21   97-8128

Published in 1997 by Harry N. Abrams, Incorporated, New York
All rights reserved. No part of the contents of this book may be reproduced
without the written permission of the publisher
Printed and bound in Japan

Harry N. Abrams, Inc.
100 Fifth Avenue
New York, N.Y. 10011
www.abramsbooks.com

Page 1: Jean Schlumberger's signature "Bird on a Rock" brooch, set with the Tiffany Diamond.

Page 2: The model in this Edward Steichen photograph in Vogue's October 15, 1940, issue wears fashion designer Omar Kiam's gold lamé dress and hair bow, and jewelry from Tiffany's display at the 1939 New York World's Fair. The ruby and diamond "Comet" brooch honored the nightly fireworks displays over the lagoon in "The World of Tomorrow" section of the fair. The diamond bracelet features an astonishingly large pink beryl or "morganite"; Tiffany's then priced the bracelet at $65,000.

Opposite: Ruth St. Denis, the founder of modern dance, with her husband and collaborator, Ted Shawn. At his celebrated 1913 Egyptian fête at Tiffany Studios in New York, Louis Comfort Tiffany presented an entertainment reenacting Marc Antony's return to Cleopatra in Alexandria. Bare-chested Nubians tossed down a bundle of rugs from which St. Denis emerged to perform her slave dance. In the foreground, a gold and enamel fringe necklace set with Montana sapphires and enamel, designed by Louis Comfort Tiffany after ancient Greek jewelry.

Page 6: Detail of an Italian Renaissance Revival teapot from the repoussé sterling silver tea service designed by Paulding Farnham for Tiffany & Co.'s exhibit at the 1904 Louisiana Purchase Exposition in St. Louis.

Table of Contents

Clockwise from upper left:

Mr. and Mrs. William R. Chaney with Paloma Picasso at the opening of the American Museum of Natural History exhibition celebrating Tiffany's 150th anniversary in 1987; William Chaney and U.S. Chief of Protocol Lucky Roosevelt at the Metropolitan Museum of Art, New York, cutting the "Magnolia Vase" cake at the opening of the Tiffany & Co. 150th anniversary show, 1987; Mr. Chaney and Elsa Peretti at Tiffany & Co., New York, to celebrate Peretti's twenty years at Tiffany's, August 28, 1994; New York Mayor Rudolph Guiliani with Mr. Chaney at Tiffany's, January 11, 1995; Broadway stars Gwen Verdon and Carol Channing with Mr. Chaney at Tiffany's, 1994; William Chaney and Audrey Hepburn at Tiffany's, August 1, 1990.

Foreword

*S*erving as chairman of Tiffany & Co. during the final years of the twentieth century, with the vast opportunities our rapidly changing world has offered, has been a unique, exhilarating and ultimately most gratifying experience.

I assumed the role of chairman in 1984 with the deepest respect for the rich heritage and the highly valued reputation that Tiffany has enjoyed as one of America's greatest institutions for over seven generations. I also came to Tiffany & Co. with a clear vision of the possibilities of an extraordinary future that would maintain the commitment to the high principles that have long guided the firm so successfully, and that could lead Tiffany to be enthusiastically welcomed by a worldwide audience.

This vision for Tiffany was of an institution firmly committed to its historic principles of providing its public with superior and innovative design, uncompromising quality, fair value, and scrupulous integrity. Given that the times were right for Tiffany & Co. to establish a wider presence in the world, we charted a confident course of expansion to many of the most prosperous cities in the United States and abroad—a course of which our founder, Charles Lewis Tiffany, a great nineteenth-century entrepreneur, would surely have been proud.

As we now approach the close of Tiffany's twentieth century, the worldwide success of that vision and of that course of action is a source of great strength, pride, and joy to Tiffany & Co.

We can say with complete confidence that Tiffany & Co. as a most uniquely American institution, has found a place in the hearts of men, women, and young people throughout the world with its ultimately distinguished products and services. For that I personally commend the people of Tiffany for their dedication and talented professionalism, and I sincerely thank our valued clientele for their loyalty and enthusiastic support.

William R. Chaney

Tiffany & Co. display case at the 1900 Exposition Universelle in Paris. Among the more important pieces, clockwise from upper left: Gold "Aztec" collar and ball pendant set with Mexican fire opals and tourmalines; diamond and gold tiara set with large American turquoises; vermeiled silver "Burmese-style" toilet set decorated with green enamel disks; pink topaz and diamond corsage ornament; "Wild Rose" brooch with a flower of pink tourmalines and diamonds, leaves of emeralds, and stems of green gold; long pendant set with Oriental pearls and diamonds in platinum; gold grapevine-motif cigarette case studded with sapphires; at center front, diamond brooch with briolette drop aquamarine pendants; the Montana sapphire "Iris" brooch now at the Walters Art Gallery in Baltimore; diamond ornament with seven black pearls. American turquoise and opal "toad" boxes with pink topaz eyes are near the lower corners of the display case.

Paulding Farnham was fond of jeweled salamanders, frogs, and toads, frequently using them to animate Tiffany & Co.'s display cases. His taste in this was not universally appreciated; the French critic Jean-Louis Bertrand in the Revue de la Bijouterie *of 1901 discussing his contemporaries' designs noted that in their quest for the beautiful and the ideal they would do well to use "moins de crapauds comme modeles" ("fewer toads as models").*

Introduction

"The year 1899 was a year of wonders, a veritable annus mirabilis, in business and production. To paraphrase a celebrated epitaph, prosperity left scarcely any of our industries untouched, and touched nothing it did not enrich." Under the headline "A Wonderful Year," *The New York Times* of Monday, January 1, 1900, waxed euphoric. "The OUTLOOK . . . uniformly hopeful and confident. The story of the nation's material progress this New Year's morning is of a nature to stir the most sluggish imagination." The nation's "public credit and its currency [are] in a sounder condition than it has known in nearly forty years. . . .We sold and exported $1,252,500,000 worth of our domestic products and our total export and import trade for the first time exceeded two billion."

The *Times* went on to note that New Yorkers had welcomed the year that "ends the nineteenth century . . . amid the din of horns and the chiming of bells.

"It would be futile to estimate the size of the crowd which made the festivities of the welcoming this new year of grace into being memorable. For certainly not in many years has such an outpouring of the people found the way to lower Broadway on a New Year's Eve.

"Not only the sidewalks, but the roadways and stoops and porticos of the big business buildings were filled. Horn-armed youths packed the streets surrounding the Trinity [Church] burying ground, and Pine Street was hardly less packed, and the crowd overflowed into Wall Street."

All was well in the world on that first day of the 1900s. America had never before known such prosperity nor had the world in general.

In the background, the original drawing and a 1900 photograph of Tiffany & Co.'s Oriental pearl, diamond, and platinum pendant, designed by Paulding Farnham for the 1900 Exposition Universelle in Paris. In the foreground, Tiffany & Co.'s 1990s pearl, diamond, and platinum "Victoria" necklace, inspired by Farnham's design.

Dia

Pex. 138

P.X. 100.

TIFFANY & CO. EXHIBIT
PARIS EXPOSITION 1900

LONG PENDANT
NEG. NO. 1905. FULL SIZE

Just over three months later, the greatest international exposition ever held would open in Paris. Celebrating the dawn of the new twentieth century, the Exposition Universelle of 1900 presented the greatest scientific, industrial, and artistic achievements of the closing years of the previous century. All offered their promises of future prosperity and achievement. America would play no small role in the great Paris Exposition. It led all nations, with the exception of the host country, France, in the number of exhibitors. Not least among those American exhibitors was Tiffany & Co., which carried home eight gold medals from the show.

Founded in 1837 by Charles Lewis Tiffany and his brother-in-law, John B. Young, with a capitalization of $1,000 advanced by Charles's father, Comfort Tiffany, the company, initially named Tiffany & Young, opened a "stationery and fancy goods" business at 259 Broadway, New York. Its first day of sales, September 21, 1837, amounted to $4.98. In 1870 Charles Lewis Tiffany's solid and inventive American entrepreneurialism brought Tiffany & Co. to a fine cast-iron Italianate palace in Union Square on the corner of Fifteenth Street and Broadway, where it reigned supreme as America's premier purveyor of jewels and timepieces as well as luxury table, personal, and household accessories. With its extraordinary success, Tiffany & Co.'s fortunes had grown from the $1,000 start-up money to a capitalization of $2,400,000, when it was incorporated in 1868. At the turn of the century, Tiffany's personal fortune was about $11 million, and the company had more than one thousand employees and branches in London, Paris, and Geneva.

Charles Lewis Tiffany held absolute faith in the idea that everything that passed through Tiffany & Co. should be not only of the finest quality of materials and craftsmanship, but of the finest quality of design as well. He also had an unerring sense of publicity and marketing; and so not surprisingly, when on March 24, 1900, Mayor Robert Van Wyck

*Above, foreground: This elaborate
Tiffany & Co. diamond and platinum
necklace, inspired by French eighteenth-century
jewelry and made about 1900, is similar to
many other diamond necklaces designed by
Paulding Farnham for Tiffany's. In the
background, photographs and hand-colored
stereoscopic slides show the East Room and the
Blue Room of the White House as decorated by
Louis Comfort Tiffany in 1882–83. President
and Mrs. McKinley held their New Year's Day
reception on January 1, 1900, in the Blue
Room with its Tiffany decor.*

*Left: The cast-iron building on Union Square
occupied by Tiffany & Co. from 1871 until
1905. Resurfaced in white brick, the building
still stands at the southwest corner of Fifteenth
Street and Union Square West.*

broke ground for the New York City subway system, in a much-publicized ceremony that opened a new era in urban transportation, it was with a beautifully crafted sterling silver spade provided by Tiffany & Co.

Charles Tiffany's exceptional taste for the rare, the fine, and the beautiful had been passed on to his son Louis Comfort Tiffany, who by 1900 was a world leader in the Art Nouveau and Arts and Crafts movements. The younger Tiffany's position as America's leading designer was established by 1882, when President Chester Alan Arthur invited him to redecorate the White House. So on January 1, 1900, when President and Mrs. William McKinley took up their places at 11:00 A.M. in the Blue Room of the White House to receive their New Year's Day guests and open Washington's social season, it was in front of a Tiffany glass-tile-faced fireplace in a decor by Louis Comfort Tiffany.

Although all but forgotten today, not enough can be said about the great fairs celebrating the turn of the century (Paris 1900, Buffalo 1901, Turin 1902, and St. Louis 1904) and the impression they made on their world.

President Loubet of France opened the great Paris Exposition Universelle around three o'clock on the afternoon of Saturday, April 14, 1900, saying, "This work of harmony, peace, and progress, however ephemeral its outward show, will not have been in vain. The peaceful meeting of the governments of the world will not be sterile. I am convinced that thanks to the persevering affirmation of certain generous thoughts with which the expiring century has resounded, the twentieth century will witness a little more fraternity and less misery of all kinds, and that ere long, perhaps, we shall have accomplished an important step in the slow evolution of the world toward happiness and of man toward humanity."

After much cheering he concluded, "It is under these auspices and in this hope that I declare open the Exposition of 1900."

The Exposition Universelle was all-encompassing in its scope and of a scale and grandeur never before imagined and never since surpassed. It covered 270 acres in the center of Paris, from the Trocadero and the Avenue de Suffren on the west to the Place de la Concorde and the Esplanade des Invalides on the east and from the Rond-Point des Champs-Élysées on the north to the Avenue de la Motte Picquet on the south. In a single year it drew 50,860,801 visitors; it was without question the greatest international gathering history has witnessed. In its boundless ambition it encompassed all human endeavor in one mammoth and dazzling-beyond-all-expectation display of art, industry, and invention.

In the words of the French novelist Paul Morand, a great parcel of the French capital was transformed into "a new and ephemeral city

Opposite, top: A Tiffany & Co. ruby, diamond, and sapphire brooch from around 1900, representing the original thirteen-star American flag.

Opposite, below: Poster for the United States Pavilion at the Paris Exposition Universelle of 1900. The French misspelled President McKinley's name and added a fourteenth stripe to the American flag.

hidden in the center of the other, a whole quarter of Paris in fancy dress, a ball, where the buildings were masqueraders. To our childish eyes, it was a marvel, a colored picture book, a cave filled by strangers with treasures."

The Paris Exposition may or may not have "accomplished an important step in the slow evolution of the world toward happiness and of man toward humanity." What it did most certainly was to give the green light to the twentieth-century principles of headlong progress in industrial production as the ultimate good and resounding financial achievement in international trade—the primary goal of all modern nations. (These of course were to be tempered—but not sidetracked—by a redeeming dosage of the arts.)

EXPOSITION DE 1900
Pavillon des Etats-Unis

Tiffany & Co. had spent several years preparing for the Exposition Universelle with the firm intention of carrying off as many medals as possible. The company was not to be disappointed. With superbly inventive and original designs by Tiffany's head designer, Paulding Farnham, Tiffany & Co. carried off not only the Grand Prize for jewelry and for silverware, but six other gold medals, two silver medals, and a bronze medal as well, underscoring the superiority and desirability of its products in the world marketplace. The firm's twentieth-century success was quite certain from the first days of 1900.

The collections to be shown in Paris had been first put on display in the Union Square, New York, store on Saturday, March 17, 1900,

A hand-colored stereoscopic view of the 1900 Paris Exposition Universelle from the Trocadero, showing the Eiffel Tower and Terrestrial Globe that inspired the Trylon and Perisphere at the 1939 World's Fair in New York; Paulding Farnham's jewelry drawings for Tiffany & Co.'s exhibit at the Paris Exposition; and a diamond and platinum lizard brooch designed by Farnham for Tiffany & Co. circa 1900, seen atop a view of the 1900 Paris Exposition from the Pont des Invalides showing, left to right, the pavilions of Turkey, the United States, Austria, Portugal, Bosnia, Persia, Hungary, Great Britain, Belgium, Luxembourg, Norway, Finland, Germany, Bulgaria, and Spain.

PX87

PX90

PX94

and were reviewed by *The New York Times* that same day:

A Representatively American Display
Private View Given

Tiffany & Co. gave a private view yesterday of their exhibit prepared for the Paris Exposition. It consists of jewelry, fancy articles and silverware. Everything was as far as possible representatively American. A number of pieces of jewelry were set with none but American stones. Among those was a beautiful corsage piece in stones of many colors, all Montana sapphires. One of the most beautiful ornaments was a collar of Roman gold studded with fire opals, with a ball pendant. It is said to form the finest collection of Mexican opals in the world.

Another rare piece was a brooch set with large black diamonds. The piece has been sold for $2,000. A beautiful diamond and emerald tiara was valued at $30,000. One of the most exquisite pieces of jewelry was a wild rose branch set in iron toned to the proper color scheme. Pink tourmalines were used together with pear-shaped emerald drops and marquise-shaped emeralds in the leaves, with diamonds and topazes to complete the flowers. Unset stones and jewels in the rough, a gold and a full silver dinner service and vases and toilet articles of beautiful design and workmanship were included in the exhibit.

Not everyone agreed as to the opening date of the new century. Germany's Emperor Wilhelm and the Empress Augusta Victoria gave a ball in Berlin on the night of December 31, 1899, to celebrate the arrival at midnight of the twentieth century, and France's Exposition Universelle of 1900 was aligned with their conviction. The United States, possibly to avoid a conflict with the Paris Exposition, elected not to recognize the arrival of a new century until January 1 of the following year. And so, following on the heels of the Paris Exposition, the

Opposite, above: Monumental gilded silver and Favrile glass punch bowl, 24" in diameter, with three ladles. Designed by Louis Comfort Tiffany, it was completed in April 1900 and shown at the 1900 Exposition Universelle in Paris and the 1902 Turin International Exposition of Modern Decorative Arts.

Opposite, below: Tiffany & Co. showed several objects derived from Native American designs at the 1900 Paris Exposition, including this silver and copper bowl. Tiffany's exposition catalogue describes the bowl as "Silver and copper. Hammered up by hand, of one piece. Shape taken from a Hupa Indian basket. Style of silver inlaying represents a flight of wild birds. The handles are conventional rattle-snakes, set with American turquoise."

United States celebrated the new century with an exposition held in Buffalo, New York, in 1901.

Tiffany's displays at the Paris Exposition had included not only the largest collection of American gems as yet assembled but a number of silver exhibition pieces based on Native American pottery and basket designs. The Pan-American Exposition in Buffalo renewed the celebratory mood of Paris while providing a new stage for American manufacturers and artists to put their wares on display and continue their promotion of superior American products on the world market.

Again Tiffany & Co. occupied a prominent position, and again its exhibits received the highest awards for jewels and jewelry as well as for silverware. As in Paris, its displays of jewelry and silverware were designed by or under the direction of Paulding Farnham. Some pieces unsold in Paris the previous year appeared again in Buffalo.

The turn-of-the-century taste for Native American design played a role in forwarding the Americanness of American products; but just what was this Americanness, and where and how did it manifest itself? One answer was to be found in the simple and significant patterns of stylized symbols and pictograms that Native Americans used to represent the natural world around them. These patterns were to greatly influence American art and design.

A number of Tiffany's designs were indigenous and clearly based on American Indian motifs, but many others, despite their concentration on American gemstones and American design, provoked confused reactions with a blend of "Viking" style silver and "Renaissance" jewels. More defensibly American styles were drawn from nature.

As France's *Revue de la Bijouterie* commented in its 1901 review of the Buffalo Exposition: "One of the characteristics of Tiffany was the concept of an exclusively American art, breaking with habits, alas!, so difficult to uproot. This idea was pushed to the most extreme limits . . . the designs, the precious metals, the gemstones used (with the exception of diamonds) and the craftsmanship are uniquely indigenous in order to realize a prototype for American art."

"Whatever," the *Revue de la Bijouterie* proclaimed, "Tiffany shined all by itself."

Did it really matter that there were strong doses of neo-Celtic interlace and neo-Renaissance arabesques along with fluted neo-classic "Pompeiian" pieces? Or if the most admired jewel in the Tiffany display was a life-size pink tourmaline carnation brooch, a flower with venerable pedigrees in Middle Eastern design, but not one that by any stretch of the imagination could be called Native American (despite its omnipresence on American lapels and in American bouquets at the turn of the century)?

There was so much to applaud in Tiffany's displays in 1901. There was the requisite promotion of the Americanness of America's designs, materials, and craftsmanship. And the originality and high level of quality of its products contributed to the perception so well expressed in a political cartoon of 1901 published in the *Detroit News Tribune* which showed a dismayed Europe guarding her negative attributes of "Lack of Invention; Old Fogyism; Lack of Enterprise; Ancient Methods; and Unprogressiveness," while Uncle Sam's starred and striped top hat comes over the horizon like the rising sun, in its rays the words "20th Century Commercial World Leader" prophesying the future.

The two great fairs of Paris and Buffalo did much to give the United States access to the world market where it would at once capture a strong and later a leading position. This new position led President McKinley to abandon nineteenth-century protectionism and to promote reciprocal trade. To that end, he went to Buffalo to speak at the Pan-American Exposition on September 6, 1901. There, while greeting admirers at the elaborate Beaux-Arts-style Temple of Music, he was

Below: In the background, a view of the Horticulture Building and Temple of Music at the 1901 Pan-American Exposition in Buffalo. In the foreground, a Baroque-style gold brooch set with natural American pearls, emeralds, and rubies and showing two nude female figures holding a pearl, designed by Paulding Farnham for Tiffany & Co.'s exhibit at the 1901 Buffalo Exposition, set atop a drawing by Farnham for a larger, Renaissance Revival pearl, emerald, sapphire, and gold brooch that was also shown in Buffalo.

Below: Tiffany & Co. chrysanthemum brooch with American freshwater pearls and diamonds set in platinum, circa 1901. Above: In the background, a view toward the Government Building at the 1901 Pan-American Exposition in Buffalo. Tiffany & Co.'s exhibit was in the Manufacturers and Liberal Arts Building, the domed structure with the American flag on the right. In the foreground, Tiffany & Co. jewelry circa 1901. Clockwise from upper left: bow-shaped gold brooch with diamonds and demantoid garnets (originally part of an important garland and bow corsage ornament designed by Paulding Farnham); heart-shaped diamond pendant; diamond bow-shaped brooch with watch pendant showing the richly pavéd diamond work favored in many of Tiffany's jewelry designs of the period; and the gold grapevine-motif cigarette case with sapphire grapes designed by Farnham that was shown at both the Paris and Buffalo expositions.

shot by an anarchist, Leon Czolgosz. Eight days later the hot-headed, rough-and-ready former governor of New York, then vice-president of the United States, Theodore Roosevelt, was sworn in as president, and the twentieth century was off and running.

One month to the day after Czolgosz fired on the American president, a simple household accident would have as dramatic and modernizing an impact on the course of Tiffany & Co. as the assassination of President McKinley had on the course of American government. On October 6, the eighty-nine-year-old Charles Lewis Tiffany fell when he attempted to put a log on the fire in the library of his country house, Tiffany Park, in Irvington-on-Hudson, north of New York City. Four days after his ninetieth birthday, on February 10, 1902, he died of complications from that fall. A struggle for artistic control of Tiffany & Co. ensued between Louis Comfort Tiffany and Paulding Farnham.

Although Farnham's designs were again shown by Tiffany & Co. at the Turin International Exposition of Modern Decorative Arts in 1902, it was clear that his irises, roses, and neo-Renaissance brooches were rapidly becoming outmoded. The committee in charge of the Turin show had decided that, as the *Jewelers' Circular Weekly* of September 24, 1902, stated, "there should be certain rigid rules prohibiting the admittance of reproductions of styles already known." Farnham's Belle Epoque revivalism, for all its brilliance, was not in sync with the new century's headlong rush toward modernism.

Tiffany & Co.'s display in the place of honor at the entrance to the Turin show was for the first time combined with that of Louis Comfort

Opposite: Original drawing for a "Burmese-style" bottle shown with a completed bottle and puff box from the toilet set of gold-plated silver decorated with green enamel plaques and studded with semiprecious gems, designed by Paulding Farnham and shown by Tiffany & Co. at the 1900 Exposition Universelle in Paris, the 1901 Pan-American Exposition in Buffalo, and the 1902 Turin International Exposition of Modern Decorative Arts. At the Paris Exposition the set comprised a comb, a dressing-table mirror, two candlesticks, a hand mirror, a puff box, two bottles, and a tray; a clock was later added.

Tiffany's Tiffany Studios and featured the younger Tiffany's naturalistic Art Nouveau lamps, Favrile glass vases, stained-glass windows, glass tiles, and enameled copper pieces. The critical and public attention these received far eclipsed that given to such works as Farnham's "Viking" coffee service, whose Celtic interlace patternings were revivalist, not modernist, in spirit. Clearly Tiffany had won the battle for artistic control of the company.

The more modern look of the straightened cleaner lines of rectilinear Art Nouveau was the keynote of the Turin show, and its influence on first the Wiener Werkstätte and in turn on the Bauhaus and Modernism cannot be underestimated.

In a telling comment, the November 1902 issue of *Dekorative Kunst*, after glowing praise of Tiffany Studios' and Tiffany's displays in Turin, mused on the unique interior of an electric kitchen shown in the American section. It was "perhaps inadvertently an excellent symbol . . . through which America had found itself in cultural life."

By 1904, Tiffany & Co.'s display at the Louisiana Purchase Exposition in St. Louis centered on an extensive collection of Louis Comfort Tiffany's naturalistic enameled and painterly jewels based on common American plants and flowers.

If the expositions at Turin and St. Louis proved anything, it was that it was time for a change. The twentieth century awoke as an age bent on one thing: Modernism.

In 1901 England's ultra-conservative Queen Victoria had died, and the Victorian order had died with her. Modern times were already in the air. That same year, no less a liberatingly post-Victorian phenomenon than ragtime jazz made its debut in the United States. The age of transportation was awakening as well. On December 17, 1903, the Wright Brothers first flew in a mechanically propelled airplane; Henry Ford marked 1903 by founding the Ford Motor Company. The year

1904 saw the first use of ultraviolet lamps, and subway trains ran under New York's Broadway. The nineteenth century, the Age of Steam as it was sometimes called, was giving way to the Age of Electricity and to ever-accelerating progress as the frontiers of science, technology, and knowledge itself expanded with dizzying speed—as they would continue to do throughout the twentieth century.

American industry and wealth were flexing their well-nourished muscles. The Union Square emporium of Charles Lewis Tiffany and Paulding Farnham was no longer adequate to accommodate a much-grown affluent segment of the marketplace nor a New York that was moving uptown.

To meet the demands of both style and the marketplace, Tiffany & Co. commissioned the great American architect Stanford White to design a new, far more palatial, and, for its time, thoroughly modern emporium, complete with the first commercial usage of stainless steel, on Fifth Avenue and Thirty-seventh Street. There Louis Comfort Tiffany, newly installed as the company's first official design director, would show the "Tiffany style" that he formerly promoted at Tiffany Studios.

The new American temple of decorative arts and industry opened its doors on September 5, 1905, moments after the close of the St. Louis Exposition. In that temple, Louis Comfort Tiffany officiated as the high priest.

And so it remained during the twentieth century. Throughout this century of abrupt change and reeling progress, Tiffany's held its own as the temple of true American style.

Tiffany's has always stood by the motto, "good design is good business," and it has succeeded and grown with that motto—and with the passion for graceful simplicity and consummate quality that is also "Tiffany style."

Tiffany & Co.'s building at the southeast corner of Thirty-seventh Street and Fifth Avenue, completed in 1905. Opposite: The exterior is marble, and the window frames, doors, and vestibules were bronze. The great American architect Stanford White of McKim, Mead and White based the exterior on the Palazzo Grimani in Venice, designed by Michele Sanmicheli in 1556. White's double-story columns make the facades appear to have three stories rather than six. Tiffany & Co. sold the building when it moved to its present Fifty-seventh Street and Fifth Avenue location in 1940. The Thirty-seventh Street building still stands and was designated a landmark by New York City's Landmarks Preservation Commission in 1988. Stanford White's color scheme for the interior (below) of the ground floor of the Thirty-seventh Street store was pearl-gray. The staircase and columns were purple-gray Formosa marble, the walls were paneled with speckled terrazzo, the teak woodwork had a soft silvery finish, the chandeliers were silver-plated, and the display cases were stainless steel in its first commercial use. Tiffany & Co.'s 1905 brochure boasted, "The elevators are the finest piece of artistic steel work in this country and place our metal workers on a level with the great smiths and forgers of the German Renaissance."

In the background, a drawing by C. S. Chapman shows Tiffany's new Thirty-seventh Street building decorated with bunting for the May 5, 1906, parade celebrating the centennial of the Seventh Regiment of the New York National Guard. In the foreground, ruby, pearl, green enamel, and gold "Holbein" pin, produced under the direction of Paulding Farnham for Tiffany & Co., after a drawing by Renaissance artist Hans Holbein (1497–1543).

Tiffany's was there to help commemorate the milestones of American culture. The Arts and Crafts movement and the opulent Art Nouveau "Tiffany style" would not survive World War I. Louis Comfort Tiffany's undulating floral and vegetable forms and tendrils and the surfaces glowing with the iridescence of age would wither in the glare of electric light and plate-glass-walled interiors. The cool, slender, debonair, and glamorous geometric forms and exquisitely pale, refined colors of Art Deco design that followed Art Nouveau would in turn be brought down to earth by the sea change of the Great Depression of the early 1930s. As the world came out of the

Jewelry designed by Louis Comfort Tiffany—from left: elaborate opal and gold necklace circa 1908, brooch with pearls circa 1910, moonstone and sapphire pendant circa 1915—against a background view of the main floor of Tiffany's store at Thirty-seventh Street and Fifth Avenue. Note the griffins supporting the display cases. They were removed in 1940 when the cases were moved to the second floor of Tiffany's present building at Fifty-seventh Street and Fifth Avenue.

Depression, streamlining, or Modernist design, triumphed in the 1939 New York World's Fair, only to be replaced by the leveling redirection of society brought about by World War II. Tiffany survived it all, as it survived the renaissance of the 1940s and the age of Hollywood; the frivolities of the postwar 1950s; the pop baroque eclecticism of the swinging 1960s; the fashion and decor mad 1970s; and the reckless, extravagant, and excessive 1980s. And Tiffany's flourishes through the anything-goes 1990s with a mixture of enthusiasm, optimism, and curiosity for what the twenty-first century will bring.

Tiffany's 20th Century documents American style at its best. It is a portrait of high style in the twentieth century as seen through the eyes of America's greatest purveyor of the trappings of the good life.

Twentieth-century Tiffany & Co. has been an essentially American institution, despite its presence in thirty-eight nations as the century closes, and it was first and foremost its sense of American design that made it that.

In 1905 Henry James wrote in *The American Scene* about Tiffany's store at Thirty-seventh Street and Fifth Avenue. His words define the Americanness of that style possibly better than it has been defined since:

> The American air . . . favors sharp effects, disengages differences, preserves lights, defines. . . .
>
> This remark was to be emphatically made in the presence of so distinct an appeal to high clearness as the great Palladian pile just erected by Messrs. Tiffany on one of the upper corners of Fifth Avenue, where it presents itself to the friendly sky with a great nobleness of white marble.
>
> One is so thankful to it for remaining within the conditions of sociable symmetry.

Tiffany design's appeal to that most important of its attributes, "high clearness," as James phrased it, distinguished it from its foreign competition. And it was Tiffany design's clean, "sharp effects"; its "disengagement" or detachment from the layerings of sophistication in design; its preservation of that key clarity and definition; its simplicity, which at times can be termed its "nobleness"; and its relaxed and "sociable" compositions that set its designs apart from the crowd.

European design in the twentieth century was, in opposition, highly sophisticated. It got that way, to state simply what was not at all simple,

Above left: A clock overlooking jewelry display cases on the main floor of the building at Fifteenth Street and Union Square, which Tiffany's occupied from 1871 until 1905 and where Farnham presided as head designer.

Left: In the background, early views of the Thirty-seventh Street store, one showing long-gone mid-nineteenth-century brownstones at the northeast corner of Thirty-seventh Street and Fifth Avenue. In the foreground, an elaborate gold bracelet set with Montana sapphires, designed by Louis Comfort Tiffany for Tiffany & Co. circa 1907, and made in the Thirty-seventh Street store's workshop.

Above: An important diamond and varicolored sapphire neo-Renaissance bracelet designed by Paulding Farnham for Tiffany & Co. shown against a background of exterior and interior views of the Union Square store.

because it had over two thousand years to evolve; and, as it evolved, it picked up a lot of baggage on its way. That baggage was loaded with religious and social (but not necessarily sociable) philosophies, political symbols, folklore vocabularies, ceremonial patterns, protocols, and conventions.

Functioning on all this received opinion in Europe produced great and, in many ways, admirable sophistication in design as in life. However, sophistication is still, for all its merits, very un-American, and it is still very un-Tiffany in both its approach and its conclusions.

American design did not have the luxury of over two thousand years to develop (Native American design aside for the moment). It had been forced to leave most of its European baggage in Europe when its founders emigrated; in fact, many of its founders were emigrating with the specific purpose of leaving that baggage behind.

To a great extent, Americans had to reinvent design from the ground up on their own terms, and reinvent it in a hurry to survive and compete in their new environment and in the world marketplace. They would reinvent it in the same way all design had been invented in the first place, by studying nature, by following their normal human desire to manipulate nature's imagery and its elements, and by following the normal human urge to take control of the environment, reordering it and abstracting it. This is precisely what design in general and Tiffany design in particular is.

The great eighteenth-century French Rococo court painter François Boucher once made the very French, very sophisticated complaint that "Nature is disorderly and badly lit." Design then might in turn be seen as the need to give nature order and clarity, to make it more understandable and less intimidating.

Throughout the later nineteenth century Tiffany design, of commercial necessity, conformed in great degree to the reigning Victorian spir-

Louis Comfort Tiffany costumed as a Middle Eastern potentate for his Egyptian fête held at Tiffany Studios, New York, on February 4, 1913. The fête, said the New York Times three days later, "eclipsed any fancy dress function ever presented in New York." Guests included John D. Rockefeller, Jr., as a Persian prince, and his wife, Abby Aldrich Rockefeller, as Minerva.

Opposite: The innovative designs of Louis Comfort Tiffany between 1900 and 1910 (clockwise from top left): Pear-shaped black opal pendant with grapevine-motif setting and chain; large enamel and gold brooch set with amethysts and opals; black opal pendant in a gold setting studded with sapphires and demantoid garnets; iridescent Favrile glass fragrance flask, its gold stopper set with varicolored gems and a central diamond; brooch set with an exceptionally fine black opal in a gold filigree setting; eighteen-karat gold ring mounted with a cabochon tourmaline; gold and enamel brooch set with American freshwater pearls. The neoclassical bronze-doré jewel casket was made by Tiffany Studios about 1910.

Left: Louis Comfort Tiffany painting in his garden at Laurelton Hall, in a 1911 portrait by the great Spanish master of light and color, Joaquín Sorolla y Bastida.

it of realism and its turgid, if sometimes Romantic, imitations of nature or of past design styles. However, fortunately for Tiffany's reputation, there was more to the story.

American designers had the bold and stylish if primitive Native American art to inspire them; and, with the opening of trade with Japan by Commodore Perry on March 31, 1854, they discovered in Japanese art—and especially in Japanese woodcuts—ideoplastic, abstract, and highly manipulated representations of nature that were quite in keeping with America's quest for clarity. Tiffany's made Japonism its own in the late nineteenth century with its great body of "Japanesque" silverware design, which remains one of Tiffany's and American design's better achievements. (Tiffany's 1871 Japanesque "Audubon" flat silver is a bestseller to this day, and its influence on Tiffany's 1990s flat silver pattern, "American Garden," is marked.) The Native American vocabulary of schematic pictographic symbols, as well as Japanese abstracted designs of nature, like similarly abstracted Egyptian hieroglyphics, were to fascinate Louis Comfort Tiffany and to further influence Tiffany design.

Above: The Tiffany family residence at the northwest corner of Seventy-second Street and Madison Avenue in New York. Designed by architect Stanford White of McKim, Mead & White, this imposing "Richardsonian Romanesque" structure was built in 1882–85 by Charles L. Tiffany for his married children. Louis Comfort Tiffany's huge studio was on the top floor, and his apartment was on the lower two floors; he inherited the building in 1902, and it was razed for an apartment house shortly after his death in 1933.

Opposite: Two remarkably modern and abstract Favrile glass vases designed by Louis Comfort Tiffany circa 1905, set against Tiffany Studios' glass mosaic tiles inspired by Native American patterns.

The organizing theme throughout *Tiffany's 20th Century* as it documents the evolution of American style and design is the urge toward abstraction, an urge as old as the cave paintings at Lascaux, the urge to discover reconciling and "significant patterns."

And that, again to simplify something that is not at all simple, brings us to the position of Tiffany design at the dawn of the twenty-first century, making its appeal to "high clearness" through significant patterns abstracted from that "best of all designers," nature.

Tiffany's twentieth-century design still speaks to us and has its success, not because of the great diversity a superficial glance sees in Tiffany's twentieth-century merchandise offerings but in the basic Tiffany design philosophy that unifies it at closer inspection. It succeeds because its eye is on the basics, not the complexities, of design.

The dazzling white marble and steel palace that Stanford White designed for Tiffany's in 1904 can be called an "abstraction" of Venetian late-Renaissance architecture. The pale limestone and polished red granite of Tiffany's current headquarters at Fifth Avenue and Fifty-seventh Street, designed in 1939 by John Cross, is even more "abstract" in its streamlined architecture of elegantly simple forms; clean lines; flat, smooth, and dapper surfaces; and harmonious proportions. Here is a clearly ordered composition, with natural materials, contrasted with stainless steel, as ornament and color. Here was the American style and the "Tiffany style" of naturally persuasive simplicity, harmony, clarity, and modernism.

Tiffany design had completed its transformation from its somewhat confusing nineteenth-century origins. It has understood its "Americanness," its

Twenty-karat gold and plique-à-jour enamel cup by Louis Comfort Tiffany circa 1914. This unique exhibition piece, which remains in the Tiffany family, was put on display in 1940 in one of the two wall vitrines at Tiffany's new Fifth Avenue and Fifty-seventh Street store. The Tiffany Diamond occupied the other vitrine, where it resides to this day. The cup with its stylized Orientalist feather and flower motifs is the most luminous and highly colored of all Louis Comfort Tiffany's pierced and enameled works. It is shown here against a background of mosaic Favrile glass panels formerly on display in the windows of Tiffany Studios, Madison Avenue at Forty-fifth Street, New York.

This trumpet-shaped, octagonal twenty-two-karat gold vase with champlevé and translucent plique-à-jour enamel lancets recalling Gothic stained-glass windows was designed by Louis Comfort Tiffany for Tiffany & Co. and completed on October 4, 1911. In the background are Favrile glass mosaic tiles from Tiffany Studios.

multiple orientations toward Europe and Asia and America's own heritage of Native American design.

Tiffany design in the twentieth century is refined rather than sophisticated, focused on simplifying nature's imagery rather than on juxtaposing and convoluting its idiosyncrasies and oppositions. Natural rather than traditional, based on observation and feeling rather than on custom and opinion, Tiffany design looks to new technologies to realize the future rather than sifting through the debris of the past for inspiration. It is not afraid of revealing and using the structural for its abstract design qualities rather than obscuring it with the purely ornamental.

It is, in its surface treatments, polished rather than textured and streamlined for action rather than statically detailed. Like contemporary Americans, it favors the media-promoted flatness of images which fall like rain on the contemporary psyche via photographs, periodicals, television, computers, and films. It is, therefore, two-dimensional rather than filled with perspectives and highlights and shadows, as in the three-dimensionality of European design.

It is notational, abstract, and linear, not unlike some of its Native American and Asiatic roots. As such, it has long departed from its figurative and painterly European antecedents.

Tiffany design is cool, direct, plainspoken as it appeals to the senses. Like all good Americans, it is economical in its means. With a nod to Henry James, we can be thankful that Tiffany's throughout the twentieth century has persisted in presenting a "sociable" design of "high clearness."

1900 – 1919

Two of the greatest designers of the decorative arts in America's history dominated Tiffany & Co. during the first two decades of the twentieth century. The first, George Paulding Farnham (1859–1927), is today all but unknown. The second, Louis Comfort Tiffany (1848–1933), is world-renowned.

Paulding Farnham's career was at its height in the very first years of the 1900s. He had become head designer of Tiffany & Co. in 1891 after the death of his predecessor Edward C. Moore, and personally designed or oversaw the design of all the great jewelry and silver collections shown by Tiffany's at international expositions from 1889 to 1904, including the Paris expositions of 1889 and 1900; the World's Columbian Exposition in Chicago in 1893; and the expositions of Buffalo in 1901; Turin in 1902; and St. Louis in 1904. His designs carried off more gold and silver medals and won more prestige in the world marketplace than those of any other American firm; how-ever,

Tiffany & Co. flower brooches designed
by Paulding Farnham.
Top: Unexecuted Farnham designs for
a lilac brooch and a wild tulip brooch
for the Paris Exposition Universelle of 1900.

TIFFANY & CO. EXHIBIT
PARIS EXPOSITION 1900
IRIS BROOCH SAPPHIRES

NEG. NO. 1903

70

FULL SIZE

TIFFANY & CO. EXHIBIT
PAN AMERICAN EXPOSITION
BUFFALO 1901

NEG. NO. 2412

Opposite, below left: Farnham's spectacular sapphire "Iris" brooch, set with 139 Montana sapphires as well as demantoid garnets and diamonds, shown by Tiffany & Co. at the Paris Exposition. The railroad magnate and art collector Henry Walters purchased the brooch at the exposition, and it is now in the museum he founded, the Walters Art Gallery in Baltimore. Opposite, below right: A preliminary drawing for a smaller iris brooch designed by Farnham for his wife, Sallie James Farnham, a sculptor best known for her 1921 equestrian statue of Simón Bolívar at the Avenue of the Americas entrance to Central Park in New York. Sallie Farnham had much admired the Walters brooch when she saw it in Paris. Above, right: The iris brooch, set with rhodolite and demantoid garnets and diamonds, that Farnham designed for his wife. To its left are a 1900 photograph of and Farnham's preliminary drawing for the Walters brooch. Left: A Tiffany & Co. pink tourmaline, demantoid garnet, and gold carnation brooch atop a photograph of Farnham's celebrated "Lawson Pink" carnation brooch that was displayed by Tiffany & Co. at the 1901 Pan-American Exposition in Buffalo.

39

even Joseph Purtell's popular history of Tiffany & Co., *The Tiffany Touch*, published in 1971, did not mention Paulding Farnham nor credit him with the great honors his works had garnered for Tiffany's and for American design.

Collaborating closely with Tiffany's eminent gemologist, George F. Kunz (1856–1932), who assembled the first and only comprehensive collections of American gemstones and pearls, Farnham created such benchmarks in the history of American design and gemology as the enameled and jeweled orchid brooches that won a gold medal at the Paris Exposition Universelle of 1889 and that first brought Tiffany & Co. prominence in the world of international jewelers.

Farnham's large-scaled flowers were his most distinctive works. His long-stemmed narcissus of diamonds, yellow sapphires, and green demantoid garnets made for the 1893 World's Columbian Exposition in Chicago; his 9½ inch-long Montana sapphire bearded iris, now featured in the Walters Art Gallery in Baltimore and possibly Tiffany & Co.'s most famous jewel; the massive wild rose corsage that received much acclaim in Paris in 1900; and the now-lost, life-sized "Lawson Pink" carnation set with pink tourmalines that was the prize of Tiffany's display at the Pan-American Exposition in Buffalo in 1901 were the first true masterpieces of American jewelry design.

His silver exhibition pieces based on Native American design were as original and masterful as his jewels and received equal acclaim. His elaborate, Neo-Renaissance gold and jeweled Adams Vase commissioned in 1893 by the American Cotton Oil Company to honor its chairman Edward Dean Adams and now at New York's Metropolitan Museum of Art attracted the universal admiration of the critics when shown at the Paris Exposition Universelle of 1900 and remains the most spectacular piece of metalwork ever created in America.

The Adams Vase. In 1893 the American Cotton Oil Company commissioned Tiffany & Co. to make a vase in honor of its chairman, Edward Dean Adams, requiring that it be "produced from materials exclusively American." Thus the yellow-green gold was mined in Forest City, California, and all the gemstones—quartzes, spessartites, amethysts, tourmalines, and freshwater pearls—came from the United States. Designed by Paulding Farnham, the vase (above) has allegorical figures representing Genius, Modesty, Agriculture, Commerce, Atlas, and Husbandry; the animals—a beaver, an owl, and a falcon—symbolize Industry, Wisdom, and Foresight.

*Opposite:
Elaborate gold and platinum brooch set with 11 American freshwater pearls, 10 Montana sapphires, and 103 diamonds, designed under Paulding Farnham's direction for Tiffany & Co.'s exhibit at the 1900 Paris Exposition Universelle; it is seen against a photograph of the entrance to the American section and the Tiffany & Co. exhibit in the exposition's Building of Furniture and Decoration.*

*Inset, top left:
The Adams Vase was the centerpiece of Tiffany & Co.'s display at the 1900 Paris Exposition, and one critic called it "a masterpiece of the goldsmith's art and a triumph for Mr. Farnham, the designer and modeller" (The Art Interchange, vol. 44, May 1900, p. 112). Now at The Metropolitan Museum of Art in New York, the Adams Vase is the most spectacular example of American metalwork ever created.*

How then could Paulding Farnham have been written out of America's design history when he is rightfully one of its greatest ornaments? His works today bring astronomical prices (an orchid pin from the Paris 1889 Exposition Universelle sold at a Sotheby's auction in October 1993 for $415,000); yet, only the most specialized student of the decorative arts would know Farnham's name.

His downfall can legitimately be seen as the work of none other than Louis Comfort Tiffany, whose tastes were far more modern and abstract than those of his father or of his father's chief designer.

Disagreement between the two began over Louis Comfort Tiffany's series of Favrile glass vases created in the pure abstract Arts and Crafts Art Nouveau style that distinguished all of Tiffany's finer work. Farnham set the vases in elaborate, figurative, Neo-Renaissance gold-and-jeweled mountings, in total opposition to Tiffany's intention. These mounted pieces, far more Farnham than Tiffany, were sent to the Paris Exposition of 1900 for all to see. It is not difficult to imagine the extreme displeasure of the great perfectionist Louis Comfort Tiffany at seeing his glass so totally denatured by another designer; however, Tiffany bided his time until the death of his father, who was at the same time Farnham's patron, before making a move. Then, in 1902, he pointedly revised a design Farnham had made for Tiffany & Co.'s "Atlas" souvenir spoon. This was a small but significant gesture.

That same year Paulding Farnham's uncle Charles T. Cook had succeeded Charles Lewis Tiffany as president of Tiffany & Co. While Cook's protection of his nephew did not stop Tiffany's son from naming himself design director and asserting a certain authority over the chief designer, it did apparently keep his annoyance with Farnham under control. All that changed on January 26, 1907, when Cook died. A few months later, Louis Comfort Tiffany moved his jewelry studio and his enameling studio into the new Tiffany building at Thirty-seventh Street

Elaborate silverwork was a hallmark of Paulding Farnham's design philosophy. This Renaissance Revival–style sterling silver vegetable dish was designed by Farnham for Tiffany & Co. and shown at the Louisiana Purchase Exposition of 1904 in St. Louis. In the background is a view of the Palace of Education at the St. Louis Exposition.

and Fifth Avenue, and on June 2, 1908, Paulding Farnham resigned from both the company and its board of directors. From that day on Louis Comfort Tiffany, America's undisputed king of the decorative arts, whose authoritarianism and luxuriant lifestyle had merited him the nickname "Kubla Khan" in his own family, reigned supreme. Paulding Farnham's masterpieces were not discussed at Tiffany & Co. for another eighty years, until 1987, when the celebration of the company's 150th anniversary encouraged a reexamination and reevaluation of the past.

Louis Comfort Tiffany's position as the world's greatest genius of glassmaking is a simple fact of the history of the decorative arts. His work as America's most innovative jewelry designer between 1907 and the United States's entry into World War I in 1917 is little known, as few of his colorful jewels so celebrated in their time have survived. In his lifetime the success and fame of his works at both Tiffany & Co. and Tiffany Studios seemed to know no bounds. If Paulding Farnham had covered Tiffany & Co. with prestige in the world market and with international critical acclaim, Louis Comfort Tiffany, with his Neo-Byzantine aesthetic and lifestyle, covered it with glory.

As the leading Louis Comfort Tiffany scholar and expert Alastair Duncan says of Tiffany's career as design director of Tiffany & Co. at the beginning of the century:

> The extraordinary growth and prosperity enjoyed by America toward the turn of the century proved fortunate for Tiffany, affording him unique opportunities to expand his business and to capitalize on the nation's first Gilded Age. The country was in a self-indulgent and self-celebratory mood, and it spent lavishly. Tiffany quickly positioned himself as its most fashionable purveyor of taste, not only within the home, but in every type of public and private institution, including churches, hotels, clubs, libraries, and hospitals. Soon his intoxicating blend of colors and designs, rendered in

Paulding Farnham, Tiffany & Co.'s chief jewelry and silver designer and the "art director" of the firm's exhibit for the 1900 Paris Exposition Universelle. He was the head designer of Tiffany & Co. from 1891 until 1902.

VASE. TIFFANY FAVRILE GLASS, GOLD AND PEARLS
NEG. NO. 1935. HEIGHT

TIFFANY & CO. EXHIBIT
PARIS EXP

Top: Louis Comfort Tiffany Favrile glass vase with Paulding Farnham's Neo-Renaissance mounting as it was shown at the 1900 Paris Exposition.
Above: Paulding Farnham's drawing for the mounted vase.

combinations of glass, bronze, enamels, and other materials became the era's proudest and most identifiable decorative imprimatur; Americans who sought to be fashionable simply could not do without it (*Louis Comfort Tiffany*, New York: Abrams, 1992, p. 13).

Ironically, Tiffany's name and his works would fall, as Farnham's had fallen, into near-total obscurity following his death at the height of the Great Depression in 1933. By then Art Deco had already reigned in the world of design for over a decade, while Tiffany had adamantly refused to move beyond the Art Nouveau style which had once made him so famous.

Louis Comfort Tiffany would, of course, enjoy a dazzling revival in the 1970s and 1980s; but, even then, his identity with his own company would be intentionally obscured by Tiffany & Co. itself with its focus on the continual modernization and progress of its design statement. This was due in part to the obvious inappropriateness of his design during the half-century following his death and due in another part to the simple fact that, despite the popularity of his products, Tiffany's obsessive perfectionism combined with the realities of the Great Depression had made his work such an unprofitable business that, by the time of his death in 1933, he had relieved Tiffany & Co. of a considerable part of its capital.

Tiffany & Co. management's express position up until the early 1980s was to disassociate itself from the works of its once principal owner and first design director. Then, like Paulding Farnham, Tiffany and his works were reevaluated in the celebration of Tiffany & Co.'s 150th anniversary. Plans were formulated to gradually produce a sizable collection of Louis Comfort Tiffany design at his former company and restate the great importance he had in building the image, renown, and merchandise offerings of Tiffany & Co. over the first third of the twentieth century.

EXPOSITION
LLAR-FIRE-OPALS

PX 42

CO. EXHIBIT
SITION 1900
RE OPALS

TIFFANY & CO. EXHIBIT
EXPOSITION 1900

PX 19.

VENDU

Left:

Paulding Farnham's drawings and photographs of his jewelry for the 1900 Paris Exposition surround the case where Tiffany & Co. displayed his creations, many of which were based on Native American designs and set with American gemstones. The Walters iris brooch can be seen at the lower left in the display case, the wild rose brooch at the lower right. Clockwise from top center: Imposing diamond and gold tiara featuring fourteen large American turquoises (the tiara's upper portion was detachable); diamond ornament set with seven black pearls, a brown pear-shaped diamond, and a yellow marquise diamond; lavishly scaled pink topaz, diamond, and pearl corsage ornament; stemmed flower brooch; diamond corsage ornament in an "Italian damask" pattern featuring six large briolette-cut aquamarines; and unset Mexican fire opals placed upon photographs and Farnham's original drawing of the gold "Aztec" collar and ball pendant, set with 45 fire opals, 14 red tourmalines, 86 varicolored tourmalines, and diamonds. (The "PX" on the drawings stood for "Paris Exposition.")

Above:

Pearl, diamond, green enamel, and gold brooch designed by Paulding Farnham, placed upon one of his drawings.

*S*terling silver and turquoise bowl based on a Zuni basket and exhibited at the 1900 Paris Exposition. One critic wrote of these pieces, "In silver articles nothing more original either in shape or in treatment could be found than the bowls, hammered out by hand from single pieces of silver, following the shapes of Zuni and Hupa Indian baskets. . . . To the artist's eye they seem better worth the thought and care bestowed upon them than the more elaborate Adams Vase" (The Art Interchange, *vol. 44, May 1900, p. 112).*

Below:
A 1900 photograph of the "Navajoe" vase.

TIFFANY & CO. EXHIBIT
PARIS EXPOSITION 1900
VASE, NAVAJOE INDIAN
NEG. NO. 1948   HEIGHT 8¾ IN

Native Americana from Tiffany & Co. against a background photograph showing the Porte Monumentale at the southwest corner of the Place de la Concorde, Paris, with Cyrus E. Dallin's equestrian statue of a Sioux warrior, Medicine Man (now in Fairmont Park, Philadelphia), at the left. Below, right, Paulding Farnham's sterling silver and copper "Aztec" bowl set with semiprecious stones, completed by Tiffany & Co. on August 31, 1905; below left, sterling silver and Arizona turquoise "Navajoe" vase, based on Navaho pottery, exhibited by Tiffany & Co. at the 1900 Paris Exposition.

NEW YORK

LONDON

TIFFANY PAVILION
INNER COURT MANUFACTURES BUILDING
PAN-AMERICAN EXPOSITION BUFFALO N.Y. 190

Left:
Tiffany & Co.'s glass-domed exhibit in the inner court of the Manufacturers Building at the 1901 Pan-American Exposition in Buffalo provides a background for a bow brooch of diamonds set in platinum, circa 1901.

Above:
Tiffany & Co. latticework seed pearl and platinum sautoir with three rose-cut diamonds; the central and pendant diamonds are surmounted by gold and enamel putti. The rose-cut diamonds and their settings were originally part of a Spanish Renaissance–style necklace designed by Paulding Farnham for Tiffany & Co.'s exhibit at the 1904 Louisiana Purchase Exposition, the only piece of jewelry by Farnham shown in St. Louis. The Craftsman noted that "the rose cut diamonds and clustering brilliants are correctly used after the manner of the sixteenth century, and the work as a whole is intended as a tour de force of craftsmanship" (vol. VII, no. 2, November 1904, p. 181). In the late 1970s, some of the Farnham elements were incorporated into a latticework pearl sautoir that Tiffany & Co. had purportedly made about 1915 for Norma Talmadge, the star of Battle Cry of Peace and Going Straight.

Above:

Tiffany & Co.'s exhibit at the entrance to the United States's section of the 1902 International Exposition of Modern Decorative Art in Turin.

Right:

"Viking" sterling silver coffee service designed by Paulding Farnham, made by Tiffany & Co. in 1901, and shown at the Buffalo Pan-American Exposition in 1901 and at Turin in 1902. The service is decorated with Celtic-derived interlace designs and enamels in pale green and lavender; it is studded with zircons and hessonite garnets.

Above:

$\mathscr{B}$ronze desk accessories designed by Louis Comfort Tiffany, made by
Tiffany Studios, and retailed by Tiffany & Co. (clockwise from left): "Ninth
Century" powder box; "Abalone" calendar; "Abalone" photograph frame; lioness
paperweight; "Zodiac" rocker blotter; "Chinese" lamp; "Abalone" clock; enamel vase;
"Chinese" paper rack; Favrile glass paperweight; "Venetian" desk blotter;
"Ninth Century" paper knife; "Venetian" magnifying glass; and glass medal.
The "Ninth Century" design has deeply incised strap work mounted with gems; the
"Abalone" design has linear, abstract grapevines with abalone-shell grapes; the "Chinese"
pattern was based on a Chou Dynasty bronze motif; and the "Venetian" pattern was based
on sixteenth-century tooled leather. The drawing of a crab is by
Agnes J. Northrop, who designed stained-glass windows
and other objects under Louis Comfort Tiffany's direction
for nearly fifty years.

Right:

Circa 1990 Tiffany & Co. gold clock set with turquoises
and corals, placed against Tiffany & Co. designs dating
from 1900 to 1910 for clocks and other objects inspired by
Native American shield patterns. The clock's design was based
on the drawing immediately to its right.

Left:

An unusual glass mosaic clock in the neo-Egyptian style,
designed by Louis Comfort Tiffany circa 1915.

A view of the Metropolitan Life Insurance Company's headquarters on New York's Madison Square serves as a background for Tiffany & Co.'s silver mechanical pencil replicas of the tower, commissioned by Metropolitan Life to commemorate the building's completion in 1909. The architect, Napoleon LeBrun, based the tower on the recently rebuilt campanile in Venice's Saint Mark's Square.

Elaborate Renaissance Revival sterling silver and crystal centerpiece designed by Paulding Farnham for Tiffany & Co. around 1904.

Above and top:

Above a photograph of the Palace of Education at the 1904 St. Louis Exposition can be seen gold and enamel samples of dandelions, held together with twine, which were part of a large collection of wildflower jewelry designed by Louis Comfort Tiffany for the Tiffany & Co. exhibit there. Gustav Stickley, the leader of America's Arts and Crafts movement, wrote of the collection, "To describe the beauty of these pieces is quite impossible. Even to picture them in black and white gives but a poor idea of their effect, which results in large measure from the color arrangement of natural stones and enamels, employed in the most skillful and varied combinations" (The Craftsman, vol. VII, no. 2, November 1904, p. 182). None of these extraordinary pieces is known to have survived.

Opposite:

$\mathcal{G}$lass tiles, scarabs, and an Egyptian-style necklace designed by Louis Comfort Tiffany circa 1909, placed against a background of Tiffany Studios' glass mosaic tiles. The necklace has thirty-six deep-blue iridescent Favrile glass scarabs set in gold, alternating with clusters of three gold balls. Louis Comfort Tiffany's personal Egyptian collection inspired several other important pieces of his jewelry, as well as less costly pieces such as scarab hat pins, scarf pins, cuff links, studs, and belts retailed by Tiffany & Co.; he believed that each piece of his jewelry "acts as a little missionary of art and tries in its own dumb way to convert the philistine" (The Art World of Louis C. Tiffany, *Garden City, N.J.: Doubleday, Page & Co., 1914*).

Above:

$\mathcal{A}$n eighteen-karat gold necklace with eleven oval citrines separated by enamel grape clusters and a pendant with a large green tourmaline, pearls, and colored diamonds, suspended from a chain of gold beads and gold-mounted pearl ornaments, both designed by Louis Comfort Tiffany circa 1907, rest on an enamel-on-copper and Favrile glass grapevine-motif plaque. Louis Comfort Tiffany devised a technique of using copper as a ground for translucent enamel to achieve iridescence similar to his Favrile glass.

ARTWORK
by
C.TIFFANY

Opposite:
Two Etruscan-style "bib neck-laces" designed by Louis Comfort Tiffany, placed upon a Favrile glass mosaic from Tiffany Studios. The necklaces were made shortly after the St. Louis Exposition, where a similar necklace won the praise of Gustav Stickley, who called it "beautiful enough to have been exhumed from a tomb at Chiusi or Volterra" (The Craftsman, vol. VII, November 1904, p. 181). The neck-lace on top has sapphire-studded ornaments and teardrop-shaped sapphire pendants; the stylized grapevine necklace on the bottom has nephrite jade grape leaves and amethyst grapes and pendants.

Above:
Louis Comfort Tiffany's famous Peacock necklace. The central medallion has a border of cabochon amethysts around a peacock mosaic of blue, black, green, and brown opals. The lappets are enameled with two peacocks, and their sapphire borders represent the peacocks' tails. Jeweled rosettes connect these elements, and an enameled wreath and a ruby are suspended beneath the medallion. The backs of the medallion and the lappets are enameled with pink flamingos. The necklace was intended for the 1904 St. Louis Exposition but was not completed in time, and it was purchased by Henry Walters sometime before 1914. In 1921—at the age of seventy-three—Walters astounded his friends by marrying his longtime companion, to whom he gave this necklace; the widowed Mrs. Walters sold it at auction in 1941.

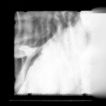

*S*tained glass by Louis
Comfort Tiffany: "Three
Seasons" folding screen
made in 1900 and exhibited
at the 1900 Paris
Exposition Universelle:
clematis representing
spring; gourds, summer;
grapes, autumn. In the right
foreground, a lampshade
with a gourd pattern on a
bronze, Moorish-style lamp,
both signed "Tiffany
Studios."

Above:

$\mathcal{A}$gainst a background of a gold leaf and Favrile glass ceiling panel atop a Favrile glass mosaic sample, both designed by Louis Comfort Tiffany for Tiffany Studios, are vases designed by Louis Comfort Tiffany circa 1904–8, with 1990s Tiffany & Co. reproductions of the vases in sterling silver. Louis Comfort Tiffany vases (left to right): three-handled ocher-glazed leaf vase; scarab bowl with a matte white glaze; two opalescent glass vases.

Opposite:

A packing box from the Louis C. Tiffany Furnaces holds a 1990s Tiffany & Co. crystal candleholder, a rare Louis Comfort Tiffany red Favrile glass vase, and a blue Favrile glass and bronze "candlestick vase." The crystal candleholder was modeled after the bronze base of the vase.

𝒜 bronze cat from Tiffany Studios draped with an Egyptian-style necklace designed by Louis Comfort Tiffany in the early 1920s, probably shortly after the November 4, 1922, discovery of King Tutankhamen's tomb. The centerpiece of the necklace is a stylized scarab with an oval turquoise body, transparent plique-à-jour enamel wings, a lapis lazuli head, gold filigree antennae, and a jade proboscis, as well as three tassels with lapis, coral, jade, and gold beads. The chain has two smaller stylized scarabs and beads of lapis, jade, coral, and gold.

Opposite:

Tiffany & Co. jewelry, designed between 1905 and 1915, placed upon Tiffany Studios' Favrile glass tiles. The stones in this jewelry do not have great intrinsic value: Julia Munson, head of Louis Comfort Tiffany's jewelry department at Tiffany & Co, later said, "Our idea was to take an inexpensive stone and bring out its natural beauty and luster by echoing its feeling in its treatment" (Quoted in Janet Zapata, The Jewelry and Enamels of Louis Comfort Tiffany, *New York: Abrams, 1993, p. 101).* Clockwise from top left: pink topaz and pearl "wreath" brooch, designed by Louis Comfort Tiffany circa 1907; pink sapphire, seed pearl, and plique-à-jour enamel necklace with a "rose window" medallion, designed by Louis Comfort Tiffany in 1907; lozenge-shaped Montana sapphire brooch designed by Louis Comfort Tiffany circa 1905; yellow beryl and blue zircon necklace with a medallion featuring a large demantoid garnet, circa 1915; eighteen-karat gold ring with zircons and sapphires, designed by Louis Comfort Tiffany circa 1910; Montana sapphire brooch designed by Louis Comfort Tiffany circa 1905.

WINGS, SET WITH OPALS. NECKLACE WITH
IOUS STONES; DESIGNED BY LOUIS C. TIFFANY

Top:
Louis Comfort
Tiffany's black
opal, demantoid
garnet, platinum, and
gold dragonfly brooch
set against a 1904 photo-
graph of some of his jewelry for
the St. Louis Exposition: an opal
and green enamel grape-motif
necklace and matching berry pin, a
sterling silver, gold, and opal dragonfly brooch with filigree wings, and a
spirea flower ornament in white enamel.
Right:
Diamond, sapphire, and gold dragonfly hair
ornament circa 1901, set against a drawing
of dandelion brooches of the same period, both
produced by Tiffany & Co. under Paulding
Farnham's direction. This dragonfly, lavishly set
with precious gems, makes a telling contrast with
the naturalistic delicacy of Louis Comfort Tiffany's
later dragonfly brooch at the top of the page.

RAWING T

Inset, right:

A photograph of the Tiffany & Co. building at Thirty-seventh Street and Fifth Avenue surrounded by a grape-motif necklace designed by Louis Comfort Tiffany for the 1904 Louisiana Purchase Exposition in St. Louis. The central grape cluster is an opal in matrix surrounded by green enamel leaves; the others are opalines. The necklace had only four opaline ornaments when Tiffany & Co. exhibited it in St. Louis and as it appears in the 1904 photograph on the facing page; Louis Comfort Tiffany later added two ornaments at the center and another at the clasp, probably when he gave the necklace to Sarah Hanley, his nurse and companion from 1910 until his death in 1933. He asked Miss Hanley to marry him, but she declined in order to avoid upsetting his children; she gave this necklace to the Metropolitan Museum of Art in New York after his death.

Three objects from Louis Comfort Tiffany's thirteen-piece exhibit in the Palace of Fine Arts, seen at left, at the 1915 Panama-Pacific World Exposition in San Francisco. The small enameled copper vase on left has motifs of mistletoe leaves with opal berries. Two of the pieces recalled Tiffany's earlier stained-glass windows in much more precious materials. On the eighteen-karat gold, six-inch-square "Four Seasons" jewel box (above), based on the "Four Seasons" window Louis Comfort Tiffany showed at the Paris, Buffalo, and Turin expositions and later installed in his country house, there are cloisonné panels for each season: a flowering cherry branch and tulips represent spring; a chestnut branch and poppies, summer; grapes and peaches, autumn; snow-covered pine branches and fire, winter. White opals, tourmalines, blue and pink sapphires, and chrysoprases surround the enamel panels. Left: The eighteen-karat gold "Tea Screen," which Louis Comfort Tiffany based on the "Parakeets and Goldfish Bowl" stained-glass window he had shown at the 1893 World's Columbian Exposition in Chicago, is pierced with openings filled with plique-à-jour, opaque, translucent, and transparent enamels. It shows a goldfish bowl and a spider web in front of a branch with parakeets and stands on a carved boxwood base.

Hand-colored postcards printed by the Pacific Novelty Co. show the 1915 Panama-Pacific International Exposition in San Francisco illuminated at night; left, the Tower of Jewels and the Central Exhibit Palace; right, the Rotunda of the Palace of Fine Arts, designed by the quirky yet masterful Bay Area architect Bernard R. Maybeck (1862–1937). The Rotunda still stands in Golden Gate Park.

This large, flared gold cup decorated with Islamic patterns in blue and turquoise plique-à-jour enamel was designed by Louis Comfort Tiffany and completed on June 13, 1913. It was shown by Louis Comfort Tiffany at the 1915 San Francisco Exposition, where Henry Walters purchased it. It is now in the Walters Art Gallery in Baltimore.

Twenty-two-inch-tall covered urn designed by Louis Comfort Tiffany for the San Francisco Exposition; the enamel decoration, based on his 1898 painting titled Spring, shows maidens honoring the goddess Flora.

TRAYNER, ALFRED
"B" Company
4th Batt. Royal Fusiliers

TIFFANY, CHARLES L.
Captain Military Intelligence
Left Tiffany & Co. 5/5/1917
Returned Tiffany & Co. 12/12/1918

SCHRAM, JOHN D.
Chief Radio Electrician U.S. Navy
Left Tiffany & Co. 4/3/1917
Returned Tiffany & Co. 4/28/1919

MOORE, LOUIS DE B.
Captain Quartermaster Corps 55th Division A.E.F.
Left Tiffany & Co. 8/ /1917
Commissioned Major 11/ /1918
Returned Tiffany & Co. 3/15/1919

KENNEDY, JAMES M.
Co. A 165th Infantry 42nd Division A.E.F.
Left Tiffany & Co. 7/10/1917
Killed in Action 7/28/1918

DISKIN, JOHN
Corporal 6th Regiment Marine Corps
Left Tiffany & Co. 5/ 1/1917
Returned Tiffany & Co. 1/13/1919

RUSSELL, JAMES
Co. A 165th Infantry 42nd Division A.E.F.
Left Tiffany & Co. 7/10/1917
Returned Tiffany & Co. 5/21/1919

Photo. International Film.

These welcomers aren't losing sleep over the danger of not getting a good place.
They have it—at 5:30 A. M.   One of many such scenes which dawn uncovered on
Fifth avenue.   Copyright, Underwood & Underwood.

SULLY, WILLARD
3rd Class Electrician Naval Reserve
Left Tiffany & Co. 5/9/1917
Did not return

O'CONNELL, NORA F.
Nurse American Red Cross
Left Tiffany & Co. 10/31/1917
Returned Tiffany & Co. 8/12/1919

DUTY HONOR COUNTRY WEST POINT MDCCCII

Opposite:

A top Tiffany & Co. drawings for United States Naval Academy rings are photographs of spectators at Tiffany's Thirty-seventh Street building awaiting the 27th Division's welcome-home parade on March 25, 1919 (center), and of Tiffany & Co. employees who served in World War I. Charles L. Tiffany, Louis Comfort Tiffany's brother, is second from left at the top. The victory parade was the New York overture to what social arbiter and commentator Elsa Maxwell wittily described as "that drunk-with-victory, torn-by-regrets and deafened-by-jazz summer of 1919" (Harper's Bazaar, November 1937, p. 88).

Above:

Photographs of World War I ace pilot Lieutenant Edward V. Rickenbacker, with Tiffany & Co.–designed bronze and silver "wings," which can be seen on Rickenbacker's collar in the photograph at the right.

Right:

The Congressional Medal of Honor as designed by Tiffany & Co. in 1917. Tiffany's designed the medal, presented as the nation's highest military award, from 1917 until 1942.

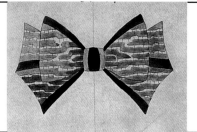

1920 - 1939

*T*he second twenty years of the century were bracketed by the great world wars, the two most devastating events civilization has encountered. The decades began, like the century itself, in a mood of near euphoria as a new social and economic order emerged from the end of World War I. Nineteen years later, they drew toward their close in a similarly optimistic mood, as faith in modern technology beckoned toward the illusion, soon to be dispelled by World War II, of a utopian future for mankind that was gloriously illustrated by the New York World's Fair of 1939.

There were, of course, some rough waters to be crossed in midstream. The Great Depression years of the early 1930s followed the stock market crash of "Black Friday." That apart, the 1920s roared in with a postwar flamboyance in spending like nothing the century had witnessed before or would see since.

The untrammeled extravagance and hedonism and the great burst of creativity that accompanied them in the postwar 1920s would eventually wear themselves out and exhaust both their financial and creative resources that had brought the nouveau riche Jazz Age and cocktail generations they championed into being; but, while almost everyone burned the candle at both ends (to paraphrase Edna St. Vincent Millay), it made a lovely sight.

In the early 1920s the United States population had edged over 100 million inhabitants. To accelerate its activities Ford Motor Company had produced its 10-millionth automobile by 1924. Westinghouse had opened the first radio broadcasting station in 1920, bringing jazz and dance music into the home, and within four years there were 2.5 million radios in the United States.

Early 1920s Tiffany & Co. design department drawings for jeweled bow brooches (left). Tiffany & Co. bow brooches on a background of 1920s drawings from the Tiffany archives (right). Throughout the 1910s, 1920s, and 1930s, Tiffany's was almost as famous for its jeweled bow pins as it was for the white satin bows on its signature blue boxes. Clockwise from upper left: a diamond, ruby, emerald, and platinum 1920s bow; a ruby and diamond bow and a diamond and sapphire bow from Tiffany & Co.'s current stock; an Art Deco rock crystal bow with diamonds and rubies; and a current diamond and gold bow.

Left:
A stylishly black-and-white Art Deco jewelry advertisement from the early 1930s serves as a background for Tiffany & Co.'s diamond and onyx jewelry of the period. Clockwise from upper right: diamond, onyx, and platinum bar pin; diamond, onyx, and platinum bracelet; diamond and platinum ring; jade, diamond, onyx, and platinum jabot pin.

Right:
Dimes and Diamonds—a 1920s F. W. Woolworth & Co. advertisement shows the affordable mass appeal of Woolworth's while gently poking fun at the aspirational, elitist appeal of Tiffany's. In the foreground, upper left, dimes; at lower right: a "streamlined" diamond and ribbed platinum Tiffany & Co. man's wristwatch of the period; and at far right, a 1920s Tiffany diamond bracelet with a fleur-de-lis pattern.

The Nineteenth Amendment was ratified in 1920, giving women the right to vote and giving the green light to the Age of Feminism, which was to continue throughout the century.

Speaking for his generation, F. Scott Fitzgerald published *Tales of the Jazz Age* and *The Beautiful and the Damned* in 1922 and in 1925 *The Great Gatsby*.

In 1927 a new world of public entertainment began as talking motion pictures made their debut with Al Jolson starring in *The Jazz Singer*. By 1928 Walt Disney would release the first Mickey Mouse films, and the first scheduled television broadcast would be made by WGY from Schenectady, New York.

Charles A. Lindbergh flew across the Atlantic Ocean in his monoplane the *Spirit of St. Louis* in 1927 to open a whole new world in long-distance transportation. In 1929 the Graf Zeppelin flew across the world from Germany to New Jersey in just over twenty days, four hours.

In the fine arts, Surrealism and Expressionism triumphed; and, in the decorative arts, the jazzy, angular linear patterns and wittily geometric stylized flowers of Art Deco ruled. In the final year of this great 1920s boom, the Museum of Modern Art opened in New York and work began on the Empire State Building. And, happily for Tiffany's, Audrey Hepburn was born.

The 1920s had been the golden age of ornamentalism, punctuated in 1925 by the Exposition des Arts Décoratifs et Industriels Modernes held in Paris. The

*Opposite, above:
In 1930 Tiffany & Co. designed and
made the eighteen-karat gold Lipton
Cup, an extraordinary tribute to the
gallantry of England's Sir Thomas
Lipton, who backed five unsuccessful
challenges for the America's Cup. After
the fifth loss, humorist Will Rogers
called on Americans to contribute to the
Lipton Cup to honor "the gamest loser in
the world of sports," and the cup is so
inscribed on the lid. Here it is
photographed at New York's South Street
Seaport with Sir Thomas's final competi-
tor, the* Shamrock V, *in the background.
Opposite, below: Sir Thomas receiving
the cup at its presentation in New York.*

*Below, right:
Drawings of the Travel and Transport
Building at the 1933–34 Century of
Progress International Exposition in
Chicago; the circular building was 200
feet in diameter and 125 feet tall.
Inset, upper left: Tiffany & Co.'s solid
platinum after-dinner coffee service,
shown at the Chicago Exposition;
comprising a tray, coffeepot, creamer,
sugar bowl and tongs, it weighed 112
troy ounces. One critic was particularly
enthusiastic about the
cut ornament:
"It seemed as if there
were studding with bril-
liants . . . so sparkling
were the pointed details"
(Owen Buttolph, "Arts of
Decoration," Spur Maga-
zine, August 1933, p. 40).
Inset, center: View of the
Federal Building at the Chicago Exposition from the Sixteenth Street Bridge. Inset,
lower right: Original ticket to the
exposition.*

United States quite rightly did not participate in this great consecration of Art Deco. American design was not on the side of ornamentalism and would have had no place in the decorative mania of Paris in 1925, where nothing was spared in the frenzy of ornament that had invaded the whole of Europe.

The critic Georges Besson wrote, "This exhibition . . . is a triumph of ornamentation, ornament at any price, rich or poor, ingenious or ridiculous, more or less openly gross, but ornament just the same."

"We protest," the great architect Le Corbusier raged, "in the name of everything. In the name of happiness and well-being, in the name of reason and culture and morality, and in the name of good taste."

The Great Depression inadvertently performed design a service by bringing all this ornamentalist silliness to a screeching halt. Then at the height of the Depression, a very different type of exposition opened in Chicago in 1933. The Chicago Century of Progress would give the world its first fleeting glimpse of a true modernist aesthetic based on twentieth-century technology.

This would be fully explored six years later at the New York World's Fair of 1939, where that greatest of all American contributions to twentieth-century design, streamlining, triumphed as the world looked enthusiastically and confidently forward in the age of speed and transportation for one brief shining moment before the world returned to chaos in World War II.

Throughout the 1920s Tiffany & Co. provided its clients at its three stores in New York, Paris, and London with the jewels, watches, smoking accessories, and stud and cuff link sets required by the party-minded Jazz Age and its newly invented café society.

Sales picked up gradually at the end of World War I. General Pershing dropped into Tiffany's Paris shop in December of 1918 to buy a diamond, pearl, and platinum bracelet for 1,130 francs. The newspaper baron Alfred Harmsworth, Viscount Northcliffe, picked out a jade and diamond watch for 1,750 francs. And, in the month of February 1919, some thirty solitaire diamond engagement rings were sold to American army officers at Tiffany's Paris branch. During the Christmas shopping season of 1919 in Paris, Singer sewing machine heiress Daisy Fellowes acquired a platinum and diamond wristwatch for 2,550 francs; Prince Poniatowski bought a pair of pearl studs weighing 28.20 grains for 9,500 francs; and the Grand Duke Alexandre of Russia, whose family had not fared so well in the war, limited himself to a diamond cross for 975 francs.

By the next year, 1920, spending was accelerating. On July 15 a St. Louis millionaire, Mr. C. J. Schmidlapp, bought a pearl choker weighing 1,383 grains for 1,460,000 francs. Chicago social queen Mrs. Potter Palmer paid 750,000 francs for a pair of Australian pearl and diamond earrings.

Retailing heir Mr. Rodman Wanamaker, who was to be Tiffany–Paris's most important client of the 1920s (Anna Gould, Duchess of

Exterior and interior views of the Tiffany & Co. Paris store on the west side of the Place de l'Opéra. The building is currently occupied by Commerzbank AG.

Exterior views of Tiffany & Co.'s old London store on Bond Street.

Below: In the 1920s Surrealist artist and photographer Man Ray invented his famous "Rayographs," abstract images made by placing objects directly onto photosensitive surfaces. This Man Ray photograph of Tiffany jewels for the 1936 Christmas issue of Harper's Bazaar *was in the style of a Rayograph. 1. A necklace of round rose-cut diamonds. 2. A black pearl and diamond ring. 3. A pair of diamond clips. 4. A yellow diamond brooch shaped like a snow crystal. 5. A pair of diamond hoop earrings.*

Talleyrand, ran a close second), made his first major purchase on October 25, 1921. He bought a necklace of eighty-one pearls for 488,700 francs. On March 13, 1923, he would spend 1,776,320 francs on pearls. Six weeks later, the duchess would buy a diamond hair ornament with two pear-shaped pearls for 188,500 francs. Pearls were the order of the day, followed by flexible diamond bracelets. No stylish woman wanted to be without both. The more conservative would settle for smaller things, but the very rich, especially the newly very rich, bought pearls, more pearls, and diamonds.

The painter Mary Cassatt would content herself with an 850-franc gold watch on October 14, 1925, and Mrs. Rudyard Kipling with a £150 sapphire and diamond bow brooch in November 1926 (she would return to Tiffany's–London the next month for a £5,900 necklace of fifty-five pearls). Mrs. Andrew Carnegie would purchase a £135 diamond bar pin and an American silver centerpiece in September of 1926. On July 31, 1925, Rodman Wanamaker would see his way clear to purchasing a 1,144,000-franc necklace of seventy-nine pearls; this was the same sum he had paid for a 13.50-carat emerald ring a few weeks before. In September he would buy an even larger pearl necklace for 1,522,400 francs, and five weeks after that, November 6, add to his collection four enormous pearls weighing 926.96 grains for 1,098,240 francs. Only Mrs. Marshall Field had outspent him on a single pearl when she bought a 77.50-grain pearl (noted in Tiffany's sales book, "with a crack") for 300,000 francs on October 8, 1924.

And so it went as the great party of the 1920s raged on to its conclusion. The last important sale of the 1920s at Tiffany's Paris branch was in January of 1929, when Mr. A. T. Fuller purchased an 18.14-carat diamond ring and a 16.82-carat emerald ring for a total of 3,890,480 francs. The next month, February 1929, total store sales for the month were only 162,242 francs. The clouds of imminent financial

Above: A whimsical publicity photograph for the April 1952 Sotheby's auction of jewelry from the estate of Hetty Wilks; right, Mrs. Wilks and her mother, Hetty Green, a shrewd investor and a good Tiffany customer who was called "the witch of Wall Street" as well as "the richest woman in America." At upper right, a Tiffany & Co. circa 1920 diamond-shaped pendant with a large central diamond and 171 old European-cut diamonds mounted in platinum.

Tiffany & Co.'s illustrious clients and its jewelry in the 1920s. In the background, clockwise from top left: Grand Duke Alexander of Russia; Anna Gould, Duchess of Talleyrand-Périgord, with her daughter Violette and two Pekinese; General John J. Pershing; Mrs. Frank J. (Florence) Gould with her Pekinese; Mr. and Mrs. Rodman Wanamaker; H.R.H. Marguerite, Duchess of Nemours. In the foreground, Tiffany & Co. 1920s ring designs and jewelry. Jewelry, left to right: cabochon emerald and diamond brooch; diamond, platinum, and gold bar brooch; diamond and platinum brooch with a large natural gray pearl; and three jeweled watches.

disaster were gathering. The Anhalt Bank had failed in Germany, and this sent a shock wave through the world financial community. Purse strings tightened.

A few good clients would come by to make modest purchases. In April 1929, General Pershing bought a 1,716-franc crystal elephant and the Duchess of Talleyrand bought a diamond and pearl ornamented compact for 1,500 francs. In August the Duchess of Nemours bought a gold "Majestic" watch for 1,850 francs and a pair of gold and enamel cuff links for 550 francs.

The New York stock market crashed two months later, and jewelry sales collapsed. In January, Tiffany's Paris store sold only three necklaces, all of them of colored stone beads, one jade, one coral, and one carnelian. In March 1930 only one necklace sold, and that of tourmaline beads. In April ten necklaces totaling over 3,500,000 francs were broken up and Paris sales totaled a mere 20,000 francs.

In London the picture was even bleaker. In the month of February 1931, Tiffany's London store made only seven sales over £15 each, and a list of "alterations of selling prices" appeared on the books starting with "Best Brooches" reduced 20 percent. By April 1931 over one-half of Tiffany–London's modest sales were accounted for by Mrs. Edward Julius Berwind, wife of the coal king of America, who bought an antique silver tea set for £166. June 1931 sales totaled just over £64; December and Christmas sales were hardly better at a mere £179. The party was over.

Although the Tiffany Diamond was featured at the Chicago Century of Progress in 1933, Tiffany's display would not center on jewels, but rather on a solid platinum after-dinner coffee set that could be easily melted down after the exposition.

Photographer Hoyningen-Huene was born in St. Petersburg in 1900 and became a highly successful commercial artist and photographer in Paris after the Russian Revolution. He abandoned Vogue *for* Harper's Bazaar *in 1935 at the behest of Harper's Alexey Brodovitch, another Russian émigré, often called "the art director of the century." Below: Hoyningen-Huene's photograph in the July 1, 1936, issue of* Harper's Bazaar *shows Ethel DuPont wearing a white calla lily dress and a Tiffany diamond bracelet and ear clips. "White," the celebrated 1930s Hollywood designer Adrian declared, "brings men to women's feet" (*Vogue, *July 1, 1937, p. 22). Not long after this photograph was taken, Miss DuPont married Franklin D. Roosevelt, Jr., the president's eldest son. Above: The pavé diamond, gold, and platinum cuff bracelet worn by Miss DuPont.*

Fashion in the mid-1930s had a penchant for aggressively colored—or as Harper's Bazaar editor Carmel Snow defined them, "shrieking loud"—plaids, with flowers and polka dots to stand up to the plaids' intensity. A collage by Ruth Sigrid Grafstrom from the May 15, 1934, issue of Vogue serves as a background for Tiffany's Art Deco jade, diamond, and sapphire jabot pin, and the diamond and gold ear clips worn by Ethel DuPont opposite.

The change of the 1930s could be seen in Tiffany's advertising. Tiffany & Co. would not reprint its great advertisement of 1920–21 that had no copy other than "Ropes of Pearls." At first there was no variance from the simple Tiffany declaration: "Quality Through Generations," "Quality Predominating," "Pearl Necklaces and Pearls for Additions to Necklaces," "Diamond Bracelets and Diamond Watch Bracelets," "Thoroughly Dependable Quality,"

"Time-Tested Standards," and "Quality Ever Foremost." The New York *Daily News Record* of June 30, 1930, stated that "Geniuses come and geniuses go, but the Tiffany manner of advertising goes on forever. Even in tough times Tiffany publicity never becomes the least bit hysterical. I have taken its blood pressure, and it does not vary" (Edward M. Ruttenberg).

Soon after, however, there was a change, not a hysterical change, but a change all the same. New York's *Advertising & Selling* of June 24, 1931, announced that "Advertising's last stronghold of chaste austerity has now been broached—henceforth Tiffany ads are to include photographs. But even in capitulation one is aware of a certain *aloof* quality. There *is* a compromise with greedy commercialism!" *Printers' Ink* chimed in on November 19, 1931, with the headline "Tiffany Goes Modern" followed by the opening line "Bring in the smelling salts!"

Throughout the 1920s, Tiffany's advertisements included only the firm's famous logo and a brief declaration, such as "Time-tested Standards," "Quality Through Generations," or the quietly grand offer of "Ropes of Pearls" made by this 1921 ad for New York's daily papers seen behind strands of pearls in this photograph. Photographic images were not used in Tiffany ads until 1931.

Only natural pearls were sold by Tiffany's until the end of the 1950s; natural pearls were generally smaller and more costly than the fine modern cultured pearls pictured here.

The ultimate in Christmas loveliness — a snowy-white fox cape with skins running vertically, from Revillon, and brilliant emerald and diamond jewels and pearls from Tiffany and Company. The emerald crêpe dress is an Yvonne Carette model, chez Revillon, the coiffure is by Martin from Vienna

T*his early Edward Steichen color photograph appeared in* Vogue's *1934 Christmas issue; the emerald green crêpe dress and white fox wrap were echoed by emerald, pearl, and diamond jewelry from Tiffany & Co. White fox was the height of fashion in 1934, but two years later* Vogue *announced "a stampede for silver fox"* (Vogue, *December 15, 1936, p. 38).*

On December 2, 1935, under the headline "Tiffany Seeks Broader Field of Customers," *Advertising Age* wrote, "Instead of the large displays of white space bearing only the name of the company, readers of local and national advertising now see straight selling copy in Tiffany space. The articles now being listed indicate that Tiffany operates an establishment where persons of modest incomes as well as those of affluence may be served."

The advertising and the price points targeted a far broader audience during the first half of the 1930s; in design, stylization verging on severity was in; lines simplified and the scale diminished.

The December issue of *Town & Country* succinctly stated the case in 1935: "The smooth despotism of the modern girl has had a chaste influence on all design. She is a completely stylized decoration herself, from her sculptured curls to the Artemis-austerity of her dinner gown. She demands the same ruthless simplification from her architect, her dressmaker and her jeweler."

Austerity began to give way to more luxuriant attitudes the next year. The Depression had eased up. In Paris the *haute couture* was booming again under the competitive leadership of Coco Chanel and Elsa Schiaparelli, and the new invention of "fashion jewelry" was emerging. *Vogue*'s December 15, 1936, issue triumphantly announced, "Dividends are being paid once more, and if you cry for your heart's desire this Christmas, you'll probably get it. Knowing women, we're betting on jewels being nearest the heart; magnificent jewels, costing a small fortune, but worth it." And so the world returned to an all-too-brief renaissance of 1920s opulence in the late 1930s.

A great celebration of the new prosperity at the dawn of the machine age was planned to open in New York in 1939. This was to be, and was, the greatest celebration of the union of art and industry, as the world accepted the inevitability of machinery and rejoiced in the facility, prosperity, and speed it brought to modern life.

Tiffany & Co. celebrated publicly with an astounding display in the fair's House of Jewels. It featured a great ruby and diamond comet brooch and a "fireworks" diamond clip honoring the advent of the aeronautic age. There was a ruby and diamond orchid brooch, lavish and sensual beyond Paulding Farnham's wildest dreams; and there was metallic jewelry in a new style of scrolling gold accented with gemstones that would lead jewelry design into the 1940s.

Tiffany celebrated 1939 privately by buying for a rumored $10,000,000 the southeast corner of Fifty-seventh Street and Fifth Avenue, where thirteen years earlier the mansion of the railroad baron Collis P. Huntington had stood; and by commissioning the architectural firm of Cross & Cross to design a fine new building in the suave and dapper streamlined American style.

Joseph Binder, a Vienna artist who had just fled the Nazi Anchluss, won the 1939 World's Fair poster contest with this design showing the Trylon and Perisphere against a night sky raked with Klieg lights; fighter planes in formation, skyscrapers, and an ocean liner complete the "World of Tomorrow" theme. In the foreground is a drawing of a Tiffany & Co. necklace of sapphires and diamonds set in gold and platinum, displayed at the World's Fair; the side elements could be detached and worn as clips.

Horst's photograph for Vogue's *December 15, 1939, issue shows a model wearing a Hudson Bay sable coat and a New York World's Fair–style emerald, diamond, and gold necklace with matching earrings pictured at the lower right.*

Designed by André Fouihoux and Wallace Harrison (two of the architects of Rockefeller Center), the 700-foot Trylon and 200-foot Perisphere at the 1939 New York World's Fair recalled the Eiffel Tower and Terrestrial Globe at the 1900 Paris Exposition Universelle. This picture of the Trylon and Perisphere under construction from Life magazine's March 13, 1939, issue shows that architectural photographs of the period were often as dramatic as the structures themselves; Dmitri Kessel used clouds lit by a setting sun to enhance the Trylon and Perisphere's otherworldly aspect. In the foreground is a Tiffany's necklace pendant with a stupendous 230-carat aquamarine from Brazil's Santa Maria mine, embellished with sapphires and diamonds, 1939–40.

Jewels
by Tiffany and Company

Left:

French Art Deco fir-tree-motif enamel cosmetic set and cigarette case studded with diamonds and rubies, from Tiffany & Co. circa 1925, atop Edward Steichen's photograph for Vogue, July 15, 1936, showing a model applying perfume from Tiffany's sterling silver streamlined American Art Deco vanity case while wearing important Tiffany diamond and colored stone bracelets.

Below: Fire and ice glamour for the April 1938 Harper's Bazaar photographed by the maverick Louise Dahl-Wolfe makes a background for two Tiffany Art Deco bracelets. Legendary fashion editor Diana Vreeland called her "passionate, ignited by her métier" (Quoted in Sally Eauclaire, Louise Dahl-Wolfe: A Retrospective Exhibition, *Washington, D.C.: National Museum of Women in the Arts, 1987, p. 9*). The surreal atmosphere may well have been inspired by the 1937 Surrealism show at New York's Museum of Modern Art and the 1938 cabaret on ice at the St. Regis Hotel's Iridium Room. The model wears a chiffon tea gown and coat by Jessie Franklin Turner, and lots of jewelry by Tiffany & Co.

• Eyes first to [...] make-up case into which the young [...]azing here. It's the latest luxury to put on [...] dressing-table—a glorified vanity-box that's completely equipped with all the beauty necessities: bottles, brush, comb, mirror, cold-cream and powder containers, jewel-case, et al. Tiffany and Company made it as well as all the jewels that the girl wears. The other attractions: a flattering head-dress of full-blown roses and a Chanel black net evening dress; both from Henri Bendel. The coiffure is by Emile of Fifty-Sixth Street.

CURRENT ATTRACTIONS

Opposite:

A ruby, diamond, and platinum cuff bracelet circa 1938 sits atop this platinum-blonde-movie-star glamour photograph by Hoyningen-Huene for Harper's Bazaar's November 1935 issue, featuring important Tiffany & Co. jewelry. The rare and splendid circa 1925 Tiffany Art Deco bracelet to the right features a stylized potted rose in rubies and emeralds on a diamond and sapphire background.

T*wo 1930s Tiffany sapphire and diamond bracelets pass behind the photograph at upper left. Below, center: An important Tiffany diamond bracelet of the early 1930s almost identical to that worn by the model on page 94.*

F*ashion and photography rose to new heights in the 1930s. Above and right: Two Edward Steichen photographs of socialites modeling summer evening dresses and Tiffany jewelry in stylish New York Deco interiors, from Vogue's May 15, 1934, issue. Steichen spent his formative years in Paris, then returned to New York in 1923 as the chief photographer for Vogue and Vanity Fair, a position he retained until 1938. He later became the Museum of Modern Art's photography director. His fashion photographs and those of several of his contemporaries straddle the border between commerce and art; they glamorize the merchandise on display, but they are also dramatic and emotional. Here Steichen used cigarettes and mirrors for a suggestive air of social drama.*

Right:

Mary Rogers (daughter of humorist and American institution Will Rogers) models Tiffany jewelry and an iridium-white lamé dress by Henri Bendel for Harper's Bazaar's December 1936 issue. The photograph was taken by Man Ray, one of the founders of the New York Dada movement in 1917; in 1921 he moved to Paris, where he became a leader of the Surrealist movement and began fashion photography for Vogue and Vanity Fair; he moved in 1934 to Harper's Bazaar at Alexey Brodovitch's urging. In the foreground are two Art Deco–inspired bracelets from Tiffany's current stock, one with sapphires and diamonds, the other all diamonds.

MÉ, MADE IN TWO PIECES WITH RHINESTONE BUTTONS

HENRI BENDEL

JEWELS ON BOTH PAGES, TIFFANY AND COMPANY

Left:

Edward Steichen's moving study of femininity for Vogue's April 15, 1936, issue. At left is a black tulle dress; at right, a light gray crêpe dress with "Anna Kareninish" ruffles by Mainbocher. All jewelry by Tiffany & Co.

Turbans were at the height of fashion in the late 1930s, and Edward Steichen undoubtedly intended the dramatic lighting of this 1937 photograph (opposite) to evoke a romantic Hollywood-style dinner in a make-believe Indian or Arabian palace. Stage and screen actress Gwili André, a favorite model of Steichen's, wore multiple bracelets, rings, and a turban clip, all from Tiffany & Co. Above: Edward Steichen photograph for Vogue highlighting important jewelry exhibited by Tiffany at the 1939–40 New York World's Fair. The vanity case and lipstick was set with 6 rubies and 46 diamonds; the bracelet (valued by Tiffany at $26,000) was set with 606 diamonds weighing a total of 74.85 carats. The diamond brooch was clipped to the hat. Four months earlier, Vogue had announced that in Paris, "New jewels glittered in many coiffures . . . jewels are all that Paris likes in hair at the moment" (Vogue, June 15, 1939, p. 23).

Right:

In this Edward Steichen photograph for Vogue, the model wears jewelry exhibited by Tiffany at the 1939–40 New York World's Fair: a diamond bracelet and four emerald and diamond clips. The clips were part of a tiara that Tiffany's made to display the 75-carat emerald now known as the "Hooker Emerald." The coiffure, dress, and hat clearly evoke film star Olivia de Havilland as Melanie in Gone With the Wind, released in 1939.

Left:

In Steichen's photograph for Vogue, August 1, 1936, Gwili André wears an ink-blue felt toque with felt "propeller" quills (inspired by Suzy, the leading Paris milliner of the day) as well as a large Tiffany star sapphire ring and dramatic gold bracelets. Star sapphires were popular for solitaire rings during the Depression, when fewer Tiffany clients could indulge themselves in large faceted precious stones. In the foreground, two Tiffany star sapphire rings from the 1930s.

Opposite, above left: Mrs. Alexander C. (I. Helen Robbins) Forbes, a second cousin of President Franklin D. Roosevelt, made her singing debut at New York's St. Regis Hotel in 1936. In this Horst photograph from Vogue's July 1, 1937, issue she is wearing Tiffany's fourteen-karat gold cuff bracelet, pictured in the foreground: it has detachable clip brooches, each set with a large cabochon emerald, three cabochon sapphires, and twenty diamonds.

Opposite, above right: In the Horst photograph from the same issue of Vogue, Dorothy Hirshon, at the time of this photograph Mrs. William Paley and one of the fashion icons to appear on Eleanor Lambert's first "Ten Best-Dressed" list, published in 1940, wears Tiffany gold bracelets to which she has added a collection of antique gold seals.

HAT AND SUIT FROM BERGDORF GOODMAN

STEICHEN

Ink-blue—new autumn rival to the almighty black—in a Descat felt toque with felt propeller quills on a real quill stalk that swoops wider than the wide lapels on the blue wool suit. Miss Gwili André is wearing a gold bracelet from Tiffany and Company

Opposite: More ink-blue in the floppy velvet hat that juts forward like a visor. You wear it with security and no elastic because of the flat, fitted back. The gold jewellery is new, too—the band bracelet and the ring, both diamond set; Tiffany and Company

Ink-blue splashes in

33

Horst's complex tableau for Vogue's *June 15, 1938,* issue: Tiffany's pear-shaped diamond ear clips and magnificent diamond clip rest on a photograph of Angelica Welldon wearing a vivid pink slouch felt hat and darker pink suede gloves by Lilly Daché; the table is strewn with flowers and a spectacular Tiffany's diamond bracelet. German-born photographer Horst began his career as the protégé of Hoyningen-Huene, although his style became more studied: as one critic noted, "Gradually introducing more imaginatively furnished sets and drapery, Horst arranged his tableaux with an eye for elegantly undulating lines and sophisticated lighting effects" (Contemporary Photographers, *New York: St. James Press, 1995, p. 508*). Two Tiffany diamond bracelets of the period are in the foreground.

Left:
Tiffany 1930s Orientalism: a colorful lapis lazuli and enamel clock with jade doors and diamond hands and numerals, placed between a pair of Han Dynasty pottery horse heads.

Below:
A 1930s Tiffany enamel clock with silver Japanese numerals, topped by a jade elephant and set on a base of black onyx and rock crystal.

In 1937, when Tiffany & Co. introduced its streamlined American Deco "Century" sterling silver flatware pattern to commemorate its one-hundredth anniversary, its advertising proclaimed, "A new flatware service of classic simplicity in the modern spirit." The pattern was reintroduced on its fiftieth anniversary in 1987, and it remains "in the modern spirit," as popular today as it was in 1937. Here a "Century" place setting is shown with matching "Century" sterling silver dinner plate, butter plate, and napkin ring, all from Tiffany's current stock. Additional "Century" flatware pieces are shown against a background of a 1937 Tiffany & Co. advertisement, below right.

Right:

Tiffany & Co. introduced its American Deco "Palmette" sterling silver flatware pattern in 1947, when a six-piece place setting cost $37.25. This pattern, whose highly stylized palm motif is reminiscent of the architectural detail lavished in the 1930s on buildings in South Beach, Miami, and in Hollywood, was also reintroduced in the late 1980s. Here a "Palmette" dessert fork, teaspoon, dinner knife, dinner fork, and butter knife from Tiffany's current stock rest atop a 1947 Tiffany advertisement.

TIFFANY & CO.
FIFTH AVENUE & 57TH STREET
NEW YORK 22, N.Y.

Price for six piece place setting including Federal Tax
Palmette pattern $37.25

Tiffany first made this still-produced sterling silver cocktail set embellished with moonstones set in gold for the 1939 World's Fair; the shaker represents a lighthouse. The hand-colored 1939 background photograph of the set includes another American Art Deco piece, a sterling silver cigarette box.

Left: Albert L. Barney, head of Tiffany's design department in the 1930s and 1940s, designed this Tiffany tea set, made of sterling silver with bakelite handles and New Zealand jade finials, in 1939; it was shown in the House of Jewels at the 1939 World's Fair. The sleek lines impart a sense of movement; the bakelite handles show the down-to-earth practicality of streamlined American Deco design.

A *1941 photograph of the special display*
room then in the northwest corner of the china and glass
floor of Tiffany & Co.'s new building at Fifty-seventh Street and
Fifth Avenue shows a table set with a centerpiece, candelabra, flat
silver, and china that had been displayed at the 1939 World's Fair.
The table's sterling silver centerpiece and three-light candelabra, which
are now in the collection of the Newark Museum in Newark, New Jersey,
can be seen in detail in the inset at upper left. Below, a sketch of one of the
red, gold, and white "Century" dinner plates that are pictured in the setting
and which were designed to complement Tiffany's "Century" flat silver.

Left:

In Louise Dahl-Wolfe's striking image from Harper's Bazaar, September 1, 1940, actress-singer Patricia Morison, who later starred in Cole Porter's 1949 hit musical Kiss Me, Kate, wears Tiffany jewels and a Schiaparelli style broad-shouldered cape. Miss Morison is standing beside an ancient Egyptian mummy from the collection of New York's Metropolitan Museum of Art.

Below: Exceptional neo-Egyptian style Tiffany bracelet from the late 1920s of diamonds, rubies, emeralds, and sapphires with the winged sun disc of the ancient Egyptian sun god Aton.

Opposite:

"A South Sea Oceanid" from Harper's Bazaar, December 1939, photographed by Hoyningen-Huene. She wears a rose-pink organza and satin sheath by Germaine Monteil and jewels by Tiffany.

Styles of all-precious stone jewelry changed little in the period, as these Tiffany bracelets demonstrate. From left, bracelet with three squares of calibré-cut diamonds and rows of sapphires and diamonds; sapphire and diamond bracelet; ruby and diamond bracelet. And below, Art Deco earrings in platinum and diamonds.

• GERMAINE MONTEIL'S SHEATH FOR A SOUTH SEA OCEANID. THE DRIFTING SKIRT IS ORGANZA, THE LONG, BONED BODICE AND SHORT-SLEEVED JACKET, NOT SHOWN, ARE SATIN. THE COLOR IS ROSE ORCHID. BONWIT TELLER. SAX-R... LOCKHARTS, ST. LOUIS. JEWELS ON BOTH PAGES FROM TIFFANY AND COMPANY.

HOYNINGEN-HUENE

Below: Tiffany's designers' preliminary drawings for tiaras to be displayed at the 1939 World's Fair; the fanciful sapphire and diamond tiara at top row center recalls the crown of the Statue of Liberty. In the center, a drawing of the emerald and diamond tiara that Tiffany & Co. made for the World's Fair to display the magnificent 75-carat square-cut emerald it had purchased at the 1911 sale of the Turkish Sultan Abdül Hamid II's property in London. The tiara could be separated into five clips (the four smaller clips are shown worn in the upper photograph on page 100). In 1950 Tiffany's reset the tiara's central emerald in a brooch, surrounding it with 109 round and 20 baguette diamonds; five years later the company sold the brooch to publishing heiress Mrs. James Stewart (Janet Annenberg) Hooker. Mrs. Hooker gave the brooch to the Smithsonian Institution's National Museum of Natural History in 1977, and the museum currently displays the "Hooker Emerald" in Tiffany's 1950 setting.

Right: Against a background photograph by Vogue's art director Anton Bruehl of Tiffany jewelry shown in the House of Jewels at the 1939 New York World's Fair, from Vogue's June 15, 1939, issue, are original working drawings for Tiffany's jewels at the World's Fair. The necklace at the center and lower right, with a huge, 200-carat aquamarine and 429 diamonds, was then valued at $28,000. The necklace above it is illustrated on page 92.

Tiffany jewelry pictured in the background display photograph, from top left: Drawing of an asymmetrical "Horn of Plenty" gold and platinum necklace set with rubies and diamonds, placed upon a postcard showing the "Helicline" ramp around the Trylon and Perisphere. Top right: Drawing of Tiffany's "Comet" brooch atop a World's Fair poster by Alice Culin; the $33,000 brooch's central stone was a pear-shaped diamond weighing 8.85 carats; there were another 218 diamonds and 104 rubies. Right: The "Fireworks" brooch had a central diamond of 8.15 carats and 266 smaller diamonds; it was valued at $43,0[...]

Center background: Tiffany & Co.'s display case in the House of Jewels at the 1939 World's Fair.

Upper right: Drawing of diamond bracelet with a massive pink beryl or "morganite," placed on a photograph of the Trylon and Perisphere taken from the courtyard of the General Motors Pavilion. Right: Drawing of the "Orchid" brooch on a photograph of the United States Pavilion; the brooch was set with 469 diamonds totaling 50.99 carats and 49 rubies totaling 12.40 carats; it was valued at $13,500. The drawings have been recreated from 1939 black-and-white photographs by Tiffany's senior jewelry designer, Maurice Galli.

4. DEC. 39

9. NOV. 39

9. NOV. 39

26. OCT. 39

A postcard of the Westinghouse Electric and Manufacturing Exhibit Building designed by Skidmore & Owings for the 1939 World's Fair in Flushing Meadows (Queens, New York) serves as a background for Tiffany's bird and flower jewelry drawings from 1939. The simplified and rather metallic style exemplified in these drawings became popular in the 1940s.

8·DEC·39

9·NOV·39

8·DEC·39

1940 – 1959

$\mathcal{A}$s the aerodynamic age celebrated its beginnings at the New York World's Fair, the first commercial transatlantic passenger flights were inaugurated by Pan American Airways' "Dixie Clipper" sea planes; and that same year, 1939, Igor Sikorsky flew the first practical, single-motor helicopter. In the United States, with no serious thought given to a coming war, Hollywood in 1939 released two of its all-time greatest films, *The Wizard of Oz* and *Gone With the Wind*. Both captured the innocent hearts and imaginations of all America. Before 1939 could draw to a close, however, Nazi Germany invaded Poland, ending the euphoria and unleashing World War II.

The twenty years between 1940 and 1960 were the greatest period of cultural change and social upheaval of the twentieth century. At the close of these chaotic decades, a mere twenty years later in 1959 in a far different world, the USSR's Luna 2 astounded the world not by crossing the Atlantic but by reaching the moon. Meanwhile, Fidel Castro reached his goal of a Communist takeover of Cuba, America's former playground, and the youth of the world dreamed of the liberated, international, and fashionably decadent lifestyle of Federico Fellini's film *La Dolce Vita*. In their turn Broadway theatergoers cheered Ethel Merman as Rose, the mother of Gypsy, in Jule Styne's musical version of the life of America's best-loved burlesque queen, Gypsy Rose Lee.

Tiffany & Co. had entered the late 1930s with the conviction that the future held all good things in store and had contracted to build a great new emporium of luxury goods; and, whether World War II raged in Europe or not, it would have to go on with its plans.

In the last weeks of 1939, on December 8 to be exact, the first of the one-hundred-ton steel trusses that would make possible a main showroom floor eighty-five by one hundred feet, unobstructed by columns, with a twenty-

four-foot ceiling height was hoisted into place at Fifty-seventh Street and Fifth Avenue. By May 8, 1940, the Indiana limestone facade of the new Tiffany building was completed; while across the Atlantic, Nazi Germany was completing the annexation of Northern Continental Europe. Tiffany's would have to largely suspend its European business (strictly speaking, the Paris office remained open, but all the jewels were locked in the vault of the Société Générale Bank).

With Germany occupying Paris and the "blitz" in full swing in London, Tiffany & Co. in New York quietly opened its new and then its only fully functioning store on Monday, October 21, 1940.

The neighboring luxury retailers, including Bergdorf Goodman, Bonwit Teller, Hattie Carnegie, and Saks Fifth Avenue, welcomed it with an ad in the *New York Herald Tribune*:

For months, the shops of the Uptown Retail Guild have watched the growth of a superb new building at the corner of Fifth Avenue and Fifty-seventh street . . . New York's most scintillating inter-section, the heart of our finest shopping center.

The boardings have now been removed and today there stands revealed a splendid structure . . . a striking example of the best in modern architecture. . . . The new home of Tiffany & Company, where are displayed the jewels and creations of the silversmith's art for which this house is famed.

Syndicated columnist Alice Hughes wrote of the opening in her October 19 by-line "Woman's New York,"

There was no band-tooting Sousa. There was no ovation by the mayor, even. The great doors were merely opened, a crowd of inter-ested persons went in without fighting, and America's most famous jewelry house was in its beautiful new home on what is undoubt-edly the world's richest "luxury corner." We New Yorkers have

Preceding pages: Stainless steel rosettes (left) at the center of Tiffany & Co.–New York's vault-like front doors, designed in 1939 by Cross & Cross. Superimposed on this time-exposed evening portrait by Ronny Jaques (right) of the Tiffany building at the busiest intersection of New York's luxury retail district, a drawing of an abstract floral brooch of emeralds and yellow and white diamonds set in gold and platinum, which Tiffany displayed at the 1939 New York World's Fair, suggests the brightly illuminated giant steel and tinsel snowflake that Tiffany's and its neighbors suspend over the crossing of Fifty-seventh Street and Fifth Avenue during the Christmas and holiday season.

Opposite, from top: In 1940 Tiffany & Co. moved from this Stanford White–designed Italianate palace at Thirty-seventh Street and Fifth Avenue to its present location. Middle: Announcing the move to Fifty-seventh Street and Fifth Avenue, this Tiffany advertisement ran on page 1 of the September 1, 1940, issue of Town & Country. *Below: Tiffany & Co.'s new Fifty-seventh Street building shortly after it opened on October 21, 1940. The architect was John Cross of Cross & Cross, whose best-known other works are the Lincoln Memorial in Washington, D.C., and the former General Electric Building at Fifty-first Street and Lexington Avenue in New York. The former GE Building, completed in 1931, is a brashly exuberant, New York Deco tower in orange brick with a neo-Gothic crown of lightning bolts symbolizing the power of electricity. The Tiffany building, on the other hand, is cool, debonair, and streamlined. Based on a classi-cal temple, it has a granite podium, a stream-lined frieze, a limestone peristyle implied by vertical rows of windows, and a cornice of highly stylized leaves along the parapet. When it was built it was criticized by traditionalists who preferred Stanford White's Thirty-seventh Street Tiffany building and by Modernists who despised all classical allusions; today, how-ever, its sleek combination of Modernism and classicism is perfectly suited to its urban con-text and Tiffany's distinctive American style.*

TIFFANY & CO.

WILL OCCUPY THEIR NEW BUILDING
EARLY IN OCTOBER

always thought of the House of Tiffany, down at 37th Street and Fifth Avenue, as something singularly permanent, like the Washington Arch or the mendicant pigeons on St. Patrick's steps.

But the swanky trade marched relentlessly further uptown, and centered in the upper Fifties, where you can see the smartest women in the smartest clothes towing the dumbest dogs. At last the old gem emporium decided to join the parade, and its lovely seven-story building is now one of the town's show places. Old-timers will rejoice that above the new door stands the Atlas-borne clock which was the hallmark of the downtown store. How many thousands of boys and girls have kept their red-hot dates "under the Tiffany clock!"

Fifth Avenue and 57th is now the dead center of the world's last remaining Gold Coast. It is our most elegant spot. It is rich, beautiful and a little overpowering. I almost curtsey to some of the sweller doormen, but then I impress easy.

On November 4, 1940, *Time Magazine* noted that, "At Manhattan's 5th Avenue and 57th Street one morning last week, two heavy glass doors revolved admitting the first of 14,000 opening-day gawkers to Tiffany & Co.'s new store. Before them in fluorescent lighted showcases lay the toniest United States jewelers' dazzling stock: diamond solitaires up to 20 1/2 carats (price: $100,000), pearls (up to $243,000 a string), emeralds, sapphires. The radiance of thousands of stones seemed to spread out and warm the visitors, an effect increased by spotlights hidden in the high soundproofed ceiling."

One Tiffany lover sent the company a poem:

> So Tiffany's moving, on with the dance
> Come Georgian silver, no back glance;
> English porcelains, take your time
> Your value now is on the climb;
> Salad bowls hurry, waddle along
> The packers will find you a box that is strong.

Diamonds, wedding rings, jump from your case,
Conscription's on, you're in the race
Canary diamond! get on your tray
J. Edgar Hoover! Take her away.

(Mrs. Joseph B. Rafferty)

So "shrouded in polite taciturnity as thick as cold chocolate sauce" (in the colorful language of *Cue Magazine*), Tiffany's moved to its present location.

In the showcase to the left of the main Fifth Avenue entrance, the astonishingly scaled jewels now returned from the World's Fair were on display: the tiara with its four detachable emerald and diamond flower clips and in the center the seventy-five-carat emerald that once adorned the belt buckle of Sultan Abdül Hamid II of Turkey; the massive morganite and diamond bracelet; the "Fireworks" brooch. In the display case to the right were the bracelet with five "extra river" diamonds of almost six carats each and other lesser jewels from the fair's House of Jewels.

Sales of such Tiffany masterpieces were rare in the war years. The great emerald would not sell until 1955, when it was purchased for $29,500 (and later donated to the Smithsonian Institution's Hall of Gems in Washington, D.C.) by newspaper heiress Janet Annenberg Hooker.

There was little to celebrate during the war. In 1941, there seemed to be only one all-American victory; Joe DiMaggio with ninety-one hits in fifty-six consecutive games set a world's record, and his teammates had Tiffany's make him a splendid silver box.

On December 2 of that year, Tiffany's published its annual jewelry selections catalogue. The most expensive item in it was a 4.42-carat emerald-cut diamond ring for a modest $6,050; the least expensive, a gold charm horseshoe and jockey cap for $4.50. Five days later, on December 7, Japan bombed Pearl Harbor, and America went to war.

Opposite:
In 1941 Joe DiMaggio had ninety-one hits in fifty-six consecutive games, sparking the New York Yankees to win the American League pennant, and setting a record that still stands in the annals of baseball. His teammates, believing—wrongly, as it turned out—that Ted Williams of the rival Boston Red Sox would be named Major League Player of the Year, commissioned a sterling silver cigarette-and-cigar box from Tiffany & Co., which they presented to Joltin' Joe as their own Player of the Year award at a boisterous celebration in the Yankees' suite at Washington's Shoreham Hotel on August 29. The cover had an engraving of DiMaggio swinging at a pitch and was inscribed "56 games . . . 91 hits"; the front was inscribed, "Presented to Joe DiMaggio by his fellow players of the New York Yankees to express their admiration for his world's consecutive game hitting record during 1941"; the players' signatures were inscribed on the vermeil lining of the cover.

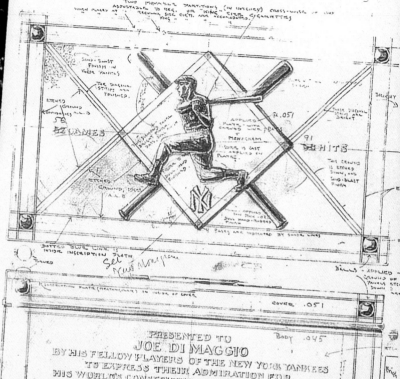

CIGARETTE BOX
'J DiMAGGIO'   ORD. 53088

PRESENTED TO
JOE DIMAGGIO
BY HIS FELLOW PLAYERS OF THE NEW YORK YANKEES
TO EXPRESS THEIR ADMIRATION FOR
HIS WORLD'S CONSECUTIVE GAME HITTING RECORD
DURING 1941

Star Gets Humidor

Special to The New York Times.

WASHINGTON, Aug. 29.—The Yankees, upon their arrival to-night from their final Western trip, staged a boisterous, impromptu celebration in honor of Joe Di-Maggio. The celebration was held to demonstrate the players' appreciation of the services of the star outfielder, who is universally credited with having provided the vital spark in the drive toward the American League pennant.

Engaging a suite in their hotel, the players, with the help of Lefty Gomez, inveigled the great DiMag to report for what was glibly described as an important signal meeting. When Jolting Joe strolled into the room, his entry was the signal for an uproarious welcome that jolted Joe right down to his convalescing sprained ankle.

Then Gomez, on behalf of his team-mates, presented to DiMaggio an ornate silver cigar and cigarette humidor commemorating the great DiMag's spectacular feat this year of setting a new consecutive hitting record of fifty-six games.

The lid of the chest reveals in bold relief the figure of Jolting Joe taking one of his famous "cuts" at the ball, with fifty-six games appearing on one side and ninety-one hits on the other.

On the front is an inscription which reads:

"Presented to Joe DiMaggio by his fellow-players of the New York Yankees to express their admiration for the world's record consecutive game hitting streak—1941."

Inside the cover on a gold, platoappear the autographs of all the Yankee players.

In making the presentation, Gomez advised his bosom pal and room-mate always to keep the chest well stocked with cigarettes. Lefty abhors cigars.

Johnny Murphy summarized the feelings of all with a toast. "We are giving this to you for your great record," he said. "You spurred us to win this pennant."

The Yanks open a two-game series here tomorrow with the Senators.

DiMaggio Gets Humidor From His Yankee Mates

By a Staff Correspondent

WASHINGTON, Aug. 29.—They say there is no sentiment in baseball, but that doesn't go for the members of New York's pennantbound Yankees. Or at least it doesn't go as far as their feeling of admiration for their great teammate, Joe DiMaggio.

Tonight in a suite at the Shoreham Joe's pals gave him a little surprise party. They gathered in the suite and then engineered with Lefty Gomez to get DiMaggio down to the apartment—and then they told him how much they respected him as a ball player and as a man and gave him a trophy to commemorate his world's record fifty-sixgame hitting streak.

"The boys dug down and cashed in a few defense bonds and bought this for you, Joe," said Lefty as he handed him a silver cigar and cigarette humidor. On the cover was an engraving of DiMaggio taking his full cut at a pitch with the record—"56 games—91 hits."

On the front of the box was the inscription: "Presented to Joe DiMaggio by his fellow players of the New York Yankees to express their admiration for the world's consecutive game hitting record—1941." Inside the cover the autographs of all his teammates are engraved.

By the holiday season of 1942, while America was trying to find comfort in Irving Berlin's new song "White Christmas," Tiffany was explaining on the top of page three in *The New York Times* that "Although our silverware manufacturing plant is devoted almost exclusively to the production of munitions of war, our stock of silverware still offers a wide selection."

In 1943 Rodgers and Hammerstein came to the rescue of America's morale with the "Oh, What a Beautiful Morning" optimistic and innocent songs of *Oklahoma!*, and Tiffany's gave up to the war effort one of the modern features of its new store in which it had taken great pride, its revolutionary central air-conditioning system.

On December 11, 1943, The Carrier Air Conditioning Co. ran a full-page ad in *The Saturday Evening Post:*

From Rubies . . . to Rubber . . . for War!

Here is an almost unknown chapter in America's war record.

It is the story of owners who voluntarily relinquished equipment—who in a very special way put aside self-interest to speed victory.

In the store of Tiffany & Company on Fifth Avenue there was a Carrier Air Conditioning System. Its heart was a Carrier Centrifugal Refrigeration Machine.

This machine was needed for the manufacture of synthetic rubber—that "America & Company" might have tires more quickly. And so Tiffany & Company permitted this essential part of their store equipment to *forsake* rubies for rubber.

In its merchandise offerings, Tiffany's would also have to forsake rubies for more affordable aquamarines, citrines, star sapphires, tourmalines, and moonstones set in the loops and leaves, cookie-cutter flowers, and bows and scrolls of polished gold that typified the 1940s.

The war would end in Europe on May 8, 1945, and in Japan on

During World War II, Tiffany & Co. did its part for the war effort. Tiffany's returned its brand-new, state-of-the-art Carrier Centrifugal Air Conditioning Refrigeration unit because it was needed for the manufacture of synthetic rubber tires for "America and Co." Carrier and Tiffany's announced this magnanimous

gesture in advertisements headed "From Rubies . . . to Rubber . . . for War!" Tiffany & Co. also turned its Belleville, New Jersey, silver manufactory into an armaments plant, produced military insignia, promoted war bonds, and saw many of its employees go off to war; several Tiffany employees who served in the war are pictured here. A 1945 Tiffany gold "V for Victory" pin sits atop the Tiffany-Carrier ad.

August 15, and America would immerse itself in a willful return to its long-lost innocence. However, a country awash in sentimentalism after the war and chanting "How Are Things in Glocca Morra?" from Harburg and Lane's *Finian's Rainbow* and "Doin' What Comes Natur'lly" from Irving Berlin's *Annie Get Your Gun* was not bent on glamour nor on luxuries such as those offered in the display cases of Tiffany & Co. Sales languished throughout the 1940s despite such encouragements to romance and gift-giving as the young and beautiful Princess Elizabeth of England's royal wedding to the handsome young Duke of Edinburgh in 1947; the re-emergence of Cole Porter's chic and worldly 1930s social values in the lyrics of *Kiss Me, Kate* in 1948; and the popularity of the hit song "Diamonds Are a Girl's Best Friend" in 1949.

Tiffany's 1949 holiday season gift selections catalogue opened with a double-page spread of "Diamonds of Fine Quality and Jewelry of Smart Design." The highest-priced diamond necklace was offered at the less-than-princely amount of $4,600. The next spread proffered "A Large Selection and a Wide Range of Price." The low-end was a stainless steel men's watch for a very modest $40. And so it went on into the 1950s.

On June 25, 1950, North Korean Communist forces crossed the 38th Parallel invading South Korea. President Truman engaged America in the conflict two days later, and yet another war began. Tiffany's would go back to turning out precision parts for anti-aircraft guns along with its silver at its Belleville, New Jersey, silver factory.

On January 31, 1953, *The Saturday Evening Post* printed the second half of an in-depth article on Tiffany & Co. written by Henry La Cossit, the war-time editor of *Collier's*. In it he concluded:

> Tiffany's is changing. It has to change. The day of the carriage trade is gone. Once there were broughams and phaetons and victorias with coachmen and footmen to help the elegant passengers alight to buy a trinket or two from the store's

Above:

E̶mlen Etting's rapid, lightly rendered fashion illustrations captured the vitality of the postwar years, when Christian Dior and Balenciaga brought luxury to Paris couture and raised high fashion's popularity to unprecedented heights. Etting came from a distinguished Philadelphia family, graduated from Harvard University in 1929, then moved to Paris to study painting; after serving as an information officer during World War II, he returned to Philadelphia and traveled extensively with his glamorous socialite wife, Boston's Gloria Braggiotti, to produce illustrated fashion and travel articles for Town & Country. *In the foreground, Tiffany & Co. buckled, fourteen-karat gold, imbricated bracelet set with diamonds and rubies, circa 1950.*

Left:

Page 1 from "Gifts from Tiffany," Tiffany's Christmas catalogue published in November 1951, pictures a solid eighteen-karat gold jewelry box, priced at $5,300, that was exhibited by Tiffany's at the New York World's Fair of 1939. A Saturday Evening Post photograph of film actress Patricia Neal wearing the catalogue's $7,850 diamond flower brooch appears on page 126.

FINE JEWELRY of the superb quality for which we have been known for many generations.

18 kt. Gold Jewel Box.................$ 5300.
Ruby and Diamond Brooch............. 4050.
Marquise Diamond Ring...............$ 13200.
Illustrations approximately ⅔ Actual Size.

Diamond Necklace..........$ 19500.
Diamond Flower Brooch..... 7850.
Ruby Ring

Oriental Pearl Necklace.......$ 31800.
Ruby and Diamond Bracelet..... 18900.
Ruby set with Diamonds........$ 13200.   13200.
Prices include Federal Tax.

Above: American Art Deco "pine cone" table centerpiece and matching candelabra designed by Tiffany's longtime director of advertising, Oscar Reedner, in 1949.

Below: Atop a Tiffany diamond jewelry ad from Town & Country, *April 1954, is an illustration of the same jewels that appeared in* The Saturday Evening Post's *January 31, 1953, issue.*

diamond counter. No more. Rolls-Royces are scarce, too; and Pierce-Arrows.

The store today is streamlined and modern, with merchandise designed for the rapid times of this mid-twentieth century; it is a store for everybody, and if any carriage trade is still around; it is still welcome along with the rest, but not with any special privileges.

. . . It is adapting itself to the world it faces.

It would be a whole new world. By 1955, "Rock Around the Clock" would be the most popular song of American youth, and Marilyn Monroe would skyrocket to fame in *The Seven-Year Itch.* The next years, the public would be immersed in Grace Metalious's *Peyton Place* and Elvis Presley would be king of rock music, with "Blue Suede Shoes," "Don't Be Cruel," and "Hound Dog" sweeping the country.

From 1907 to 1914, Tiffany's earned an average of $1,077,759 a year. This had dropped in mid-century to an average of $323,530 a year for the eleven years up to 1954.

In 1955 Walter Hoving, whose Hoving Corporation controlled Tiffany's Fifth Avenue neighbor Bonwit Teller, bought the controlling interest in Tiffany & Co. from various members of the Tiffany family for $3,765,384.18. That year the store's net income had settled at a mere $172,600.

Hoving began a comprehensive rehabilitation program of marking down and cleaning out slow-moving merchandise and of redecorating the entire Fifth Avenue store. His "great white elephant sale" of 1956 brought profits down to $140,009; but his merchandising initiatives paid off, and by 1957 profits were up again to $251,445. They would be double that in three more years.

To help in the resuscitation of Tiffany & Co., Hoving wisely decided to reinstate the office of design director, which had been vacant since the departure of Louis Comfort Tiffany. He called upon his old friend the distinguished former president of the Parsons School of Design, Van Day Truex.

Truex immediately recommended that Tiffany's hire the world's best-known jewelry designer, French-born Jean Schlumberger. On February 17, 1956, Hoving bought the assets of Schlumberger Inc. for Tiffany's.

On March 23, the *New York Journal American* reported on Tiffany's new designer: "'Some women want to look expensive, I would prefer to have them look precious,' stated Jean Schlumberger, famed creator of jewels. Today he has been honored by the United States. Tiffany & Co., that landmark of tradition in the world of jewels, has given him his own department in their store." (Barbara Bruce)

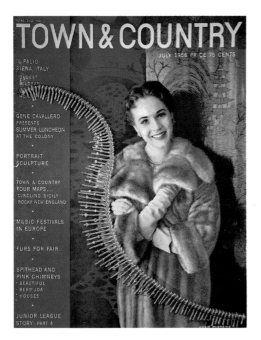

In the September 1956 issue of *Harper's Bazaar,* it was reported that "Jean Schlumberger's designs, like those of his Renaissance predecessors, have their own mythology—of fairy-tale beasts and jewel-crusted sea creatures, and of flowerings . . . never seen outside the herbarium of his imagination, each a marvel of the jeweler's art."

Whatever they were, Schlumberger's idiosyncratic, witty, lavish, and ever-so-stylish jewels that had sprung from the late 1930s Surrealist group that surrounded the great Paris fashion designer and Schlumberger's first patron, Elsa Schiaparelli, were then, and remain forty-some years later, the pride of Tiffany & Co. Four months after Schlumberger's arrival at Tiffany's in July of 1956, Hoving saw to it that a Schlumberger necklace appeared on the cover of *Town & Country* modeled by none other than Broadway's newest and brightest star, Julie Andrews, who was conquering New York in *My Fair Lady.*

Hoving introduced other changes. He brought his resident wizard of window display at Bonwit Teller, Gene Moore, to reinvent Tiffany's windows. Gene Moore's supremely witty and often surrealistic visual echoes, teasing contrasts of rough versus smooth, and Lewis Carrollian shifting-scaled whimsy not only brought added fame to the grand old house of Tiffany's but reinvented retail window display for the whole world. Moore would stay on at Tiffany's until 1995, and he remains the universally acknowledged world leader of window display.

In 1958, Hoving set the jewelry industry on its haunches once again by breaking with Tiffany tradition and offering Tiffany's clients fine cultured pearls. Tiffany's was back in the business of offering "Ropes of Pearls," this time marketable to a broader audience. By the end of the 1950s, Walter Hoving's Tiffany's was again on center stage.

• The vitriolic note of poison green—hard, fresh, and biting.

• Above . . . in a Jane Derby dress of silk faille

trimmed with inserted zigzags and jagged points of black lace—

Against a background of a fashion illustration by Takal for the September 1, 1940, issue of Harper's Bazaar centering on a chair of scrolling forms popular in the jewelry of the 1940s sits a Tiffany gold bracelet of the period. Toned down red, white, blue, and gold color combinations were a mark of the early World War II years. The war-influenced slate blue, introduced by Molyneux, was a popular color of the time. Schiaparelli had her own, darker, war-influenced "Maginot blue," which combined well with her still-popular pale cerise or "Parlor pink."

Left:
An emerald and diamond bracelet and bow from Tiffany & Co. circa 1940 on top of a fashion illustration in Harper's Bazaar's September 15, 1940, issue, which announced "The Call to Colors . . . bright Irish green, magnificent at night with emeralds and diamonds. . . . And, for a quick, clean break across lush nights, the bright violence of POISON GREEN." The drawing was made by Hungarian-born artist Marcel Vertès just as the Nazis entered Paris; although Vertès was in the French army stationed north of Paris, he continued to supply fashion illustrations to Harper's Bazaar and maintained his sense of humor. Harper's December 1939 issue described Vertès's army life in a delicious parody of Ernest Hemingway's prose style: "He decided to give a party for the men in his regiment. He made wall brackets for candles out of tree branches. He washed the walls and decorated them with charcoal pictures of naked women."

PAIR OF 14 KT. GOLD AND SAPPHIRE EARRINGS
14 KT. GOLD BRACELET .... $ 145.
50.

Top left:
Tiffany & Co.'s 1940s gold bracelet with three large
emerald-cut peridots weighing fifty-four carats and round dia-
monds set in gold scrolls.

Above: A Tiffany & Co. gold bracelet from the mid-1940s, priced
at $50, placed upon a Tiffany ad that appeared in Harper's Bazaar
in October 1947; a drawing of the bracelet is at the center.

Left: A brooch featuring an emerald-cut citrine with "rays" of old European-
cut diamonds, set in undulations of pink and yellow gold, Tiffany's circa 1940.

Opposite: A matching suite comprising a necklace, a bracelet, and a pair of earrings
with large emerald-cut citrines and rubies set in eighteen-karat gold scrolls, from
Tiffany's circa 1940. In the background are newspaper advertisements from the 1940s
for similar jewels using other large emerald-cut colored gemstones.

$\mathcal{J}$ean Schlumberger, one of the founding fathers of fashion jewelry, began his career as a jewelry designer working for Elsa Schiaparelli in 1936. After serving with the Free French Forces during World War II, he moved to New York in 1947 to open his own jewelry store. In March 1956, Tiffany chairman Walter Hoving persuaded Schlumberger to join Tiffany's as a vice-president with his own semi-separate shop at Tiffany's. Schlumberger's intricate, colorful jewelry, inspired by nature's idiosyncrasies, was avidly collected by discerning socialites, and it has remained in fashion to this day. He told a reporter in 1961: "Modern jewelry has become flat. It's designed to show off value before beauty, before elegance. It says: 'Look at me. I'm rich. I'm loved. I'm important.' I don't believe in that. I'm trying to make jewelry which is as close as possible to a woman's personality and as wearable as possible" (New York Post, November 10, 1961, p. 50).

Below: Three Schlumberger brooches are placed adjacent to their drawings; they are, from left, "Arrows," gold set with amethysts, sapphires, and diamonds; "Seahorse," eighteen-karat gold and platinum set with peridots and diamonds; and "Beribboned Crown of Thorns," gold

and platinum set with a morganite and canary and white diamonds. Schlumberger made the "Arrows" and "Crown of Thorns" brooches in 1947–48 for Standard Oil heiress Millicent Rogers, pictured above; a strikingly beautiful socialite, Mrs. Rogers was on the list of Best-dressed Women year after year; she also assembled an important collection of Native American art, now the Millicent Rogers Museum of Northern New Mexico in Taos, where she lived during the 1940s and 1950s.

Opposite, far left:

Gypsy Rose Lee, the greatest burlesque queen of all time. Her second husband, William Alexander Kirkland, gave her the pair of Mexican fire opal Tiffany bracelets (in the foreground and above) on January 9, 1954, her fortieth birthday. The Aztec motifs of these bracelets recall the "Aztec" fire opal necklace that Tiffany & Co. displayed at the 1900 Exposition Universelle in Paris; like the necklace, they were undoubtedly designed by Paulding Farnham.

Below, clockwise from top left: Fashion designer Elsa Schiaparelli, the first to promote the jewelry designs of Jean Schlumberger; Elsie de Wolfe, whose panache made her the most successful interior decorator of the century; and Daisy Fellowes, a French aristocrat as well as a Singer sewing machine heiress, who was famous for her biting wit, extravagance, and chic—Elsa Maxwell called her "the most fascinating and easily the most glamorous human being I have ever met" (Harper's Bazaar, November 1937, p. 133). In December 1939 Elsie de Wolfe—by then Lady Mendl—gave a luncheon at her villa in Versailles; the guests included Mme Schiaparelli and the Hon. Mrs. Reginald Fellowes, who wore a stem and leaf brooch (shown here at center) designed by Jean Schlumberger to hold a real rose blossom. Another luncheon guest, Louise Macy, described it in Harper's Bazaar: "I've never before seen anything so lovely—truly a masterpiece. . . . The leaves are red and green enamel—they open to show the veins inside, which are tiny bands of rubies and diamonds and pale blue enamel" (Harper's Bazaar, December 1939, p. 128). In the foreground, rose jewelry drawings by Schlumberger.

Charity balls became leading social events in the 1950s. Right: Tiffany & Co.'s citrine and diamond necklace made in Paris in the 1950s, superimposed on a photograph of the 1956 April in Paris Ball at New York's Waldorf-Astoria Hotel; Elsa Maxwell, who organized the annual charity event, is at center wearing gold lamé and seated next to her frequent companion, Prince Aly Khan. Background and opposite: Tiffany & Co. sponsored the Tiffany Ball, held on July 13, 1957, at Marble House in Newport to raise money for the Preservation Society of Newport County. In the background, the canopied terrace outside the ballroom at Marble House. Inset photographs opposite, clockwise from upper right: John F. Kennedy, freshman U.S. Senator from Massachusetts; Mrs. John R. (Noreen) Drexel, III, greeting Senator and Mrs. Kennedy; Mrs. Sheldon Whitehouse, honorary chairman of the ball, wearing the famous Tiffany Diamond in a setting designed by Jean Schlumberger; Perle Mesta, Washington party-giver ("the hostess with the mostest") and former Ambassador to Luxembourg, whose career inspired Irving Berlin's Broadway musical Call Me Madam, starring Ethel Merman; the gold ballroom at Marble House with the Tiffany Ball in progress. Charles L. Tiffany bought the 128.51-carat Tiffany Diamond in 1879, shortly after it was unearthed in South Africa's Kimberly Mines, and he put it on display at Tiffany's. After Walter Hoving took over Tiffany's he toyed with the idea of setting the diamond, which had never been worn, pricing it at $582,000. He lent it to Mrs. Whitehouse for the Tiffany Ball. When the ball ended at 4 A.M., she turned it over to two Tiffany guards, one of whom told a reporter, "She gave it back right there in front of everybody at Marble House. Why not? Everyone knew that one wasn't hers" (New York Times, July 16, 1957).

Lanvin

Marie-Blanc
Lanvin

Jean de
COUNTESS
POLIGNAC

This Emlen Etting sketch appeared in the September 1949 issue of Town & Country; Gloria Braggiotti Etting described the occasion: "Comtesse Charles de Polignac, daughter of the late Jeanne Lanvin, gave an intimate party at her own residence to show a selected group of dresses from her new collection which is also her first. . . . As we sat in her salons, hung with Vuillards, Bonnards, and Renoirs . . . the models, holding roses in their hands, synchronized their steps to amplified recordings of Brahms' waltzes and 'Amor' by Monteverdi with Nadia Boulanger at the piano and Comtesse de Polignac singing." In the foreground, Tiffany & Co.'s generously proportioned pussy willow spray brooch circa 1950; oval cabochon moonstones represent catkins and small diamonds represent nubs on the branches.

Below: A Tiffany & Co. gold hobnail bracelet set with diamonds and matching earrings circa 1950, placed upon a fashion illustration of the 1950s by Guillermo Bolin.

Bolin

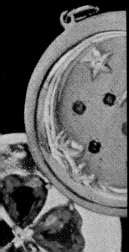

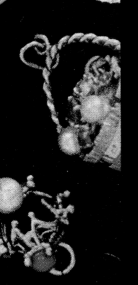

Left:
own & Country's *November 1954*
photograph of bracelets and charms from Tiffany
& Co. and other jewelers serves as a background for a
Tiffany & Co. gold bracelet with American gold coins,
made specially for World War II and Korean War hero Admiral
Joseph James Clark and presented to Mrs. Clark on Christmas 1954.
Above: An important Tiffany woven eighteen-karat gold passementerie
necklace from the 1950s, placed upon a Serge Matta illustration
of the period executed as a silk scarf by the Paris fashion house
of Jacques Fath. The Chilean-born Matta, a brother of
famous abstract Surrealist artist Roberto Matta, drew
witty illustrations for both Jacques Fath and Elsa
Schiaparelli.

$\mathscr{R}$ené Bouché drawings of 1950s high society paired with Tiffany jewelry of the period. Opposite, above: A Tiffany two-flower brooch of emeralds and diamonds set in platinum and gold. Bouché's drawing shows sophisticated revelers at the El Morocco, New York's chicest nightclub in the 1950s. Opposite, below: A Bouché drawing of the Palm Court at New York's Plaza Hotel, a popular luncheon watering hole of 1950s society, serves as a background for a Tiffany floral bouquet brooch and matching earrings; the flowers are made of lapis lazuli, carnelian, chalcedony, and dyed and clear rock crystal, with diamond stamens and gold pistils.

Above: Bouché's drawing of an elegant and eminently 1950s woman in an eminently 1950s sedan wearing a black dress and long white kid gloves, with a 1990s Tiffany pendant necklace and matching earrings of diamonds set in platinum, in the enduring style popularized in the 1950s by Maurice Galli, now Tiffany's senior jewelry designer.

president of the Hoving
-opening of the Waldorf-
nd was patterned after
lk of Paris last winter

Preceding pages: Jean Schlumberger's jewelry drawings serve as a background for photographs of his jewelry and some of its notable collectors. *Above, left:* Socialite Mrs. Harrison (Mona) Williams, arriving with Ben Ali Haggin and Cecil Beaton at the Metropolitan Opera Ball on April 28, 1933; and some years later wearing Schlumberger's "Cascade" brooch while talking with Schlumberger and Brazilian-born socialite Vera Plunkett. Mona Williams was a quintessential American beauty. In 1927 interior decorator Elsie de Wolfe asked Elsa Maxwell to her Villa Trianon at Versailles "to see something beautiful," and Miss Maxwell later recalled, "I anticipated a full-sized thrill. I was not disappointed. . . . Facing me was a woman with a beautiful figure and the eyes of an amazed child" (Harper's Bazaar, November 1937). *Right:* Mona Williams talking to Walter Hoving during the Bal des Oiseaux at the Waldorf-Astoria's Starlight Roof in June 1949. *Center, below:* Mr. and Mrs. William S. Paley with the Duchess of Windsor and Milton Holder at a benefit for the North Shore Hospital on November 11, 1955. The always exquisitely dressed and glamorous Babe Paley is wearing Schlumberger's turquoise, diamond, and eighteen-karat gold "Tassel" necklace, the drawing for which is at the upper right.

Below, left: John Loring arriving at a party in the 1970s with legendary fashion priestess Diana Vreeland, who was one of Schlumberger's most avid supporters from the very outset of his career. She was well positioned to support and publicize her designer friends in her successive roles as editor of Harper's Bazaar and of Vogue. Schlumberger designed one of his finest jewels, the trophy brooch, for Mrs. Vreeland. The drawing for this unusual jewel can be seen at the top center of page 132.

Below: René Bouché's late-1950s drawing of Elaine Lorillard, cofounder of the Newport Jazz Festival, serves as a background for Schlumberger's extravagant, complex "Flowers" bracelet of pearls and diamonds in platinum and eighteen-karat gold, made for Vera Plunkett, who is pictured with Mona Williams on page 144.

Opposite:

The model in this extraordinary June 1957 Vogue photograph wears the Tiffany jewelry designed by Jean Schlumberger shown in the foreground: "Cooper" bracelet of diamonds set in platinum and eighteen-karat gold, "Morning Glory" earrings of sapphires and diamonds in platinum and eighteen-karat gold, and, at the waist of the dress by Philip Hulitar, "Sombrero" clip of sapphires and diamonds in platinum and eighteen-karat gold. Vogue declared: "Surprise without an ounce of shock to it: melon-yellow chiffon for summer evenings. Surprise on the side: bright melon-colouring for lips and fingernails."

Opposite:

Jean Schlumberger's diamond, platinum, and eighteen-karat gold "Star" brooch for Tiffany & Co., superimposed upon a 1956 Town & Country photograph of Mrs. Winston ("C.Z.") Guest wearing a Tiffany necklace by Schlumberger and a mink jacket by Mainbocher. Long celebrated as the most beautiful of America's social figures, Mrs. Guest has recently won further acclaim for her practical gardening advice in the New York Post.

Above: Irving Penn's photograph for Vogue's June 1957 cover: the model wears the Tiffany jewelry designed by Schlumberger shown in the foreground—"Multiplication" emerald and eighteen-karat gold ear clips, and "X" bracelet of pavé diamonds in platinum connected by eighteen-karat gold chains.

Left: Lavish late-1950s Tiffany & Co. jeweled gold compact.

149

Tiffany jewelry from the late 1950s atop Serge Matta's whimsical gallery drawings of the period.

Opposite: Kay Thompson, film actress, cabaret singer, and author of the ever-popular "Eloise" children's books, selects accessories in her role as the Diana Vreeland–like fashion editor in the 1956 Audrey Hepburn and Fred Astaire movie Funny Face. *Jewelry, left to right: sapphire and diamond paisley brooch; eighteen-karat gold charm bracelet; diamond, emerald, sapphire, and gold "Starfish" brooch; fourteen-karat gold necklace.*

Above: A French schoolboy in his sailor suit, who is innocent of the world of fashion accessories and would undoubtedly prefer a hoop to roll down the streets of Paris to the gold coil necklace pictured.

Below: Tiffany's "Engaging Idea!" diamond ring advertisement from the late 1950s inevitably recalls Marilyn Monroe's breathy rendition of "Diamonds Are a Girl's Best Friend" in Howard Hawks's 1953 film Gentlemen Prefer Blondes.
Above, center: An array of important solitaire rings set with marquise-cut diamonds.
opposite, below right: Tiffany's "Make a Wish" ad with a pear-shaped diamond engagement ring on the winning portion of a wishbone.

Engaging Idea!

TIFFANY & CO.

Make a wish

Leonard Lyons, in his New York Post gossip column, "The Lyons Den," made the wildly unrealistic suggestion on October 5, 1959, that the "Tiffany Diamond, whose price tag is $500,000, would be only a down payment if Marilyn Monroe will do the film version of Breakfast at Tiffany's. Producer Marty Juro has tax experts working on the diamond-plus-percentage deal. . . ." Fortunately for Tiffany's, Juro chose Audrey Hepburn, who did not at all share in the "Diamonds Are a Girl's Best Friend" philosophy, to star in his film.

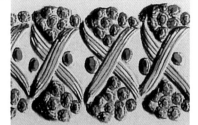
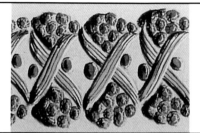

The twenty years between 1960 and 1980 were the golden age of the Hoving epoch at Tiffany & Co. The first year of the period saw Tiffany profits back up to a then very healthy $570,080. Encouraged by the success of his remake of Tiffany's, Walter Hoving on June 16, 1960, announced his resignation as both president of the Hoving Corporation and chairman of Bonwit Teller in order to devote full time to Tiffany's.

Although the Hoving Corporation controlled Tiffany's, it in turn was controlled by Genesco, Inc., whose principal business was footwear and ready-to-wear apparel. Both Maxey Jarman, Genesco's chairman, and Hoving had grown to find the fit uncomfortable between the two companies. Hoving, then already sixty-three years old, regrouped his financial forces and on October 27, 1961, bought 52 percent of Tiffany's stock for a little less than $6 million.

Walter Hoving had had a varied but brilliant retail career, having served, beginning in 1928, as vice-president of R.H. Macy & Co., at thirty-four years old as vice-president of Montgomery Ward & Co., at thirty-eight as president and chairman of Lord & Taylor, and at forty-three as president and chairman of Bonwit Teller. He would remain chairman of Tiffany & Co. from September 15, 1955, until his retirement at age eighty-three in 1981. Along the way, he had been awarded the Legion of Honor by the French government on February 4, 1952, and had served as the president of the Salvation Army Association of New York for twenty-one years, retiring on December 15, 1959, with the farewell words, "Let me paraphrase Mary Martin in her song 'My Heart Belongs to Daddy.' My heart will always belong to the Salvation Army."

His "trade-up, not trade-down" merchandising philosophy saved Tiffany & Co. from the downward slide of the decade between the end of World War II in 1945 and his taking control of the troubled company in 1955.

Five *brooches by Jean Schlumberger are displayed on a background of Schlumberger bracelet drawings. Clockwise from center: "Gazelle," head of pavé diamonds with gold horns and emerald eyes; "Cascade," a flowering plant in pavé diamonds cascading over a large yellow sapphire; an eighteen-karat gold "Camel" with a pearl headdress, platinum collar, lapis lazuli hump, and rubelite ornaments; "Wings," a large peridot with four clusters of sapphires, carried by four diamond wings; and "Floral," a cabochon emerald surrounded by leaf sprays of diamonds set in eighteen-karat gold and platinum.*

Two fanciful aquatic-motif brooches by Jean Schlumberger are shown against an Art Deco illustration of the underwater plant Saccorhiza bulbosa: "Meduse" brooch (above right), a diamond and moonstone crown with tentacles of eighteen-karat gold and sapphires set in platinum, and "Pegasus" (below), a flying seahorse with a body of emeralds and pavé diamonds, wings of eighteen-karat gold, amethyst eyes, and a "mane" of round-cut diamonds.

Left:
Walter Hoving, chairman of Tiffany & Co. from 1955 to 1981, as photographed for Business Week's October 6, 1962, cover story: "Urbane showman, thoroughgoing merchandiser, with a dash of crusader thrown in, Hoving believes Tiffany can lead public taste to new levels. He's gambling that there's a bigger market for taste—Tiffany taste of course."

Tanzania to Tiffan

From the foothills
Mt. Kilimanjaro c
Tanzanite, the lovelie
gemstone discovered in over
Tanzanite can now be found
quantities in only two pl
world. In Tanzania. And

Right: Tiffany scion Henry B. Platt escorts Elsa Maxwell, longtime ringleader of café society, to the opening of the exhibition of Schlumberger's jewelry at Wildenstein & Co., New York, November 1, 1961.

Below: Walter Hoving, Jean Schlumberger, and First Lady Jacqueline Kennedy also attended the opening of the Schlumberger exhibit at Wildenstein & Co.

Hoving's trading-up was paying off. In 1961 profits jumped to $782,000 on sales of $13.4 million. When asked why department and specialty stores were vigorously trading down in the unprecedented prosperity at the end of the 1950s, he replied that merchandising responsibilities were increasingly being entrusted to "bright young men from business schools who should have been statisticians instead of merchants." "Merchants," he commented, "need courage; statisticians don't."

The new chairman knew just how to restore Tiffany's luster and prestige. In 1961 he held an exhibition of Schlumberger jewelry at Wildenstein & Co., New York's most prestigious art gallery. He made sure that his good friend from Newport, America's new and adored First Lady, Jacqueline Kennedy, would attend. He encouraged his director of Tiffany's jewelry division and Louis Comfort Tiffany's great-grandson socialite Henry B. Platt, to escort Elsa Maxwell, the elderly founder and arbiter of café society, to the Wildenstein opening. Schlumberger sales doubled.

Design and, as he called it, "aesthetic excitement," always came first for Walter Hoving. When asked in an interview published in the

Rings by Tiffany designer, Donald Claflin.

DESIGNS COPYRIGHTED TIFFANY & CO. 3

Nature yields a new gem to the world. Named Tanzanite by Tiffany, after the country of origin, it is the most beautiful blue stone discovered in over 2,000 years.

3

Tanzania to Tiffany's

Until two years ago, the location of a tiny pocket of blue gemstones was known only to a group of primitive Masai tribesmen in Tanzania. The stones had lain there for millions of years, hidden in the foothills of Africa's Mt. Kilimanjaro, a setting as rich in natural beauty as the gems themselves.

Then, as in many great discoveries, circumstances brought these rare stones to light and the attention of one of our senior officers. He named them Tanzanite.

Recognizing Tanzanite as the loveliest blue gemstone discovered in over 2000 years, he immediately enlisted the talents of our designers and craftsmen to create the world's first great collection of Tanzanite jewelry.

Today, Tanzanite can be found in significant quantities in only two places in the world.

In Tanzania. And Tiffany's.

TIFFANY & CO.

NEW YORK FIFTH AVE. AND 57TH ST.
CHICAGO 715 NORTH MICHIGAN AVE. · HOUSTON FIRST CITY NAT'L BANK BLDG. · SAN FRANCISCO 252 GRANT AVE. · BEVERLY HILLS WILSHIRE BLVD.

Above: In 1967 Henry B. Platt, a great-grandson of Louis Comfort Tiffany and later president and chairman of Tiffany & Co., learned that Masai tribesmen had discovered blue gemstones approaching the beauty of sapphires near Africa's Mount Kilimanjaro. Platt negotiated Tiffany's exclusive marketing rights for the stones from the newly independent nation of Tanzania and named them tanzanites. Tiffany's first introduced the tanzanites at its San Francisco store in October 1968, calling them "the most beautiful blue stones discovered in over 2,000 years." Unset tanzanites, with Paloma Picasso's diamond ribbon and tanzanite pin and a Tiffany & Co. pear-shaped tanzanite and diamond pendant, are seen here against pages of Tiffany's tanzanite promotional materials. *Left:* "Harry" Platt with his frequent companion, the Duchess of Uzès, the former Peggy Bancroft, December 1977. *Top:* Harry Platt and Aileen Mehle ("Suzy," the undisputed queen of society columnists) at one of Platt's biennial Christmas dinner dances, at the St. Regis Hotel's Versailles Suite, New York, November 1979.

November 18, 1962, *New York Times Magazine* how he felt America could best compete with ever-popular foreign imports, he replied:

In my opinion, the situation requires a new approach. It requires the creation of a new profession which will function midway between the top management and the designing staff. In my judgment, it requires a "design editor"—one who will set design policy, the design point of view.

He should be a "specialized" designer but should have an intimate knowledge of design in many fields. He must be a person with a broad cultural background and what is commonly called taste. . . . Top management, which is used to formulating policy in production, marketing and finance, must come to realize that policy must also be decided upon in the field of design, and carried out just as consistently. . . . "Price" is not the only factor involved in being aggressively competitive. To be competitive in design is no less important.

In Van Day Truex, Tiffany's design director for the twenty-three years from 1956 until 1979, Hoving had found the ideal arbiter of taste for Tiffany & Co.

"Mr. Truex," said the *New York Herald Tribune* of December 8, 1960, "directs the design and styling of Tiffany's . . . and when it comes to the question of taste he's splendidly opinionated, emphatically outspoken and dead right.

"He's for positive designs, whether they're plain or elaborate, that are personal and look as though they were made for an individual rather than for the statistics on mass taste."

Truex would distinguish himself by completely redesigning Tiffany's china, crystal, and silver merchandise in the late 1950s

Opposite:
Louis Comfort Tiffany had based some of his jewelry designs on weeds such as dandelions and Queen Anne's lace; Van Day Truex expanded on this tradition by basing Tiffany & Co. objects on common articles of everyday use. His "Strawberry Box" was made of vermeiled sterling silver, yet it was otherwise an exact replica of throwaway wooden boxes used for selling berries in grocery stores. This Midas-like transformation also had Dadaist and Surrealist aspects, recalling Marcel Duchamp's "ready-mades," such as the snow shovel he displayed as a work of art.

Opposite, below:
Van Day Truex, Tiffany's design director from 1956 to 1979, spent his formative years as an artist and art teacher at the Parsons School of Design in Paris between the wars. Like Louis Comfort Tiffany, Truex often looked to nature for inspiration, saying, "Every designer should take himself to the [Natural History] Museum and look at the bugs and the butterflies and shells. Nature is still the best designer" (New York Herald Tribune, *December 8, 1960).*

and 1960s. His "Bamboo" flat silver and silver giftware candlesticks, plates, and bowls would win international design awards.

In April 1960 President Eisenhower gave President and Mme de Gaulle of France a table centerpiece of four of Truex's silver "Bamboo" candlesticks and a silver "Bamboo" bowl. Two months later, Eisenhower gave the young king and queen of Thailand a pair of vermeiled seed-pod-shaped Tiffany tureens also designed by Van Day Truex.

Always a consummate publicist and marketer, Walter Hoving knew that his friendship with President Eisenhower could pay off handsomely in publicity for Tiffany & Co. When the president came to Tiffany's to make a pendant that Eisenhower had designed as a 1955 Christmas gift for his wife, Mamie, he asked Hoving whether the president of the United States gets a discount at Tiffany & Co. "Well, Abraham Lincoln didn't," was Hoving's reply, alluding to some pearl jewelry that Lincoln had bought at Tiffany's in 1861 for $530. Eisenhower did not get a discount, but Hoving got ample publicity by repeating the now-legendary story to the press.

Hoving's greatest publicity coup was allowing sequences of the movie version of Truman Capote's *Breakfast at Tiffany's* starring Audrey Hepburn to be filmed in Tiffany's itself. *The New York Herald Tribune* of Monday, October 3, 1960, described the event:

The conversion of Tiffany's into a movie set began at 5:30 P.M. Saturday when the store closed for the week-end. A ten-man crew worked until midnight constructing camera platforms, setting up lights and covering the hardwood aisles with rolls of brown wrapping paper to prevent scratches.

At 7 A.M. yesterday the job was continued. A half hour later Miss Hepburn, coffee container in one hand and a sugar twist in the other, stepped from a cab in a black evening gown and strolled past Tiffany's in the breakfast scene that explains the title.

Opposite: **S**urrealists in the 1920s were fascinated by Karl Blossfeldt's photographs of unusual plant forms, and Van Day Truex based Tiffany's sterling silver "Seed Pod" centerpiece on Blossfeldt's photo of the fruit of Blumenbachia Hieronymi, *a rare Argentinean loasa. Here Truex's centerpiece is placed in front of Blossfeldt's photograph. President & Mrs. Dwight D. Eisenhower presented a pair of Truex's "Seed Pod" centerpieces to King Bhumibol Adulyadej and Queen Sikrit of Thailand on their state visit to Washington, D.C., in June 1960. Opposite, above: The queen, the first lady, the king, and the president pose for photographers before a state dinner at the Mayflower Hotel on June 30, 1960. Below: President and Mrs. Eisenhower at one of the four inaugural balls held on the evening of Ike's second inauguration, January 20, 1957. Bottom: Mamie Eisenhower wearing the gold medallion with a five-pointed star circled by a holly wreath designed for her by the president and made by Tiffany & Co. The front of the pendant was inscribed "To Mamie"; the back, "For never failing help since 1916—in calm and in stress, in dark days and in bright. Love, Ike. Christmas, 1955." Mrs. Eisenhower violated a White House family rule against disclosing who gave what to whom by proudly displaying the pendant to reporters and photographers on Christmas Day.*

The next year *Breakfast at Tiffany's* would be released, and Tiffany's would achieve a place in the world's imagination that it had never previously known. Audrey Hepburn, as well as the film's theme song, Henry Mancini's and Johnny Mercer's "Moon River," would become forever associated with Tiffany & Co.

Twenty-six years later, for Tiffany's 150th anniversary, Miss Hepburn wrote a note to preface the book *Tiffany's 150 Years:*

Dear Tiffany,

A thing of beauty
is a joy *forever*
that is why the lustre
of the art of Tiffany's
remains undimmed.

For 150 years your name
has stood for beauty
        style
        quality
        and constancy
you have brightened our faces
        with your jewelry
illumined our homes
        with your lamps
brought a glow to our
        tables with your silver
given distinction to our lives,
you certainly have to mine by
inviting me to breakfast—how many
can say they've had coffee and
croissants at Tiffany's?—a memory
I shall always cherish.

Happy Birthday, dear T.,
with love—but also with envy,
for after 150 years you don't
have a wrinkle—but then, class
doesn't age!

Your devoted friend,
Audrey Hepburn

Above:
Prominent socialite *Lyn Revson holding a gold basket-work minaudière and wearing an enamel and eighteen-karat gold bracelet, both designed by Jean Schlumberger for Tiffany & Co.*

Louis Comfort Tiffany's great-grandson "Harry" *Platt putting Jean Schlumberger's gold and diamond ribbon necklace with the Tiffany Diamond at its center on film star Audrey Hepburn for a Tiffany & Co. publicity photograph made at the time of the filming of* Breakfast at Tiffany's *on October 2, 1960.*

Top:

When Mrs. Lyndon B. Johnson commissioned Tiffany & Co. to design a new
dinner service for the White House, Tiffany's
design director Van Day Truex based the decoration on "Lady Bird" Johnson's beloved
American wildflowers, with stylized American
eagle motifs from President James Monroe's
service on the larger pieces. The center of each
dessert plate has a different state flower,
painted by Tiffany artist André Piette in the
style of early nineteenth-century botanical
watercolors. In all, there are ninety different
wildflowers on the 2,190-piece service. In the
photograph above, Mrs. Johnson poses with
the new dinner service for the Ladies' Home
Journal in June 1968; above right, the service
as displayed in the Ladies' Home Journal
article.

And so the design and publicity tri-
umphs of the 1960s continued. In
1968, Tiffany & Co. would make a
new china dinner service for President and Mrs.
Lyndon B. Johnson. The new White House china designed by
Van Day Truex and André Piette would feature the American
wildflowers dear to the heart of the First Lady.

Shortly afterward Henry B. Platt named and introduced the
jewelry world to tanzanite, the first "new" blue gemstone to be
discovered in over two thousand years. It became almost a
Tiffany trademark. Five years later, Platt would name and intro-
duce yet another gemstone, tsavorite, a green garnet also found
in Tanzania.

Left:

Saul Leiter's Harper's Bazaar, *December 1966, photograph of Donald Claflin's walrus brooch in gold with ivory tusks, light blue enamel jacket with pavé diamond collar and cuffs, dark blue enamel trousers, and white enamel vest. The little girl holding the brooch is presumably having a Lewis Carrollian dream of Alice's oyster-loving walrus in* Alice in Wonderland.

Opposite:
René Bouché fashion illustrations from the early 1960s serve as backgrounds for jewelry designed by Donald Claflin for Tiffany's. Left, fanciful animal brooches (clockwise from upper right): the walrus brooch; yellow enamel and turquoise frog with cabochon emerald eyes and pavé diamond feet and eyebrows; double ram's head with horns of carved lapis lazuli, a gold and diamond head, and emerald eyes; winged dragon in pavé diamonds, with a ruby tongue and emerald eyes, curled around a turquoise. Right: A disk brooch of ivory studded with turquoises, varicolored gems, and gold beads, designed by Claflin for Tiffany & Co. circa 1965.

While Jean Schlumberger jewels became the definitive status symbol of the 1960s, another remarkably talented designer, Donald Claflin, would be brought to Tiffany's to add his own fabulous jeweled birds and beasts and flowers and starbursts to the eclectic-to-neo-Baroque design vocabulary of the 1960s. Hoving, aided by Platt, would see to it through their extraordinarily adept press relations that no American fashion magazine would be published without full-page illustrations showing either Schlumberger or Claflin jewels.

Tiffany's international expansion began in 1972. President Richard Nixon had recently returned from his historic visit to Russia and China when he received a letter from Hoving:

September 28, 1972

Dear Mr. President:

Knowing your interest in the balance of trade with Japan and your efforts to improve this for the U.S.A., you will be interested to know that good old Tiffany's has just made an agreement to export American diamond jewelry to Japan. We have shipped this week over a half million dollars of diamonds and other jewelry to Japan and expect to send several hundred thousand dollars more in the next few weeks.

This may be a drop in the balance-of-trade bucket, but at least it's in the right direction.

Pauline and I are praying for your re-election at our prayer time every morning.

Warmly,

Walter

One month before the election, Nixon replied:

October 5, 1972

Dear Walter:

Your diamond export business to Japan may be just in its early stage of development, but knowing you as I do, I am certain you will soon be making a significant contribution to our balance of payments!

With deep appreciation to Pauline and you for your prayers and with warm regards to you both,

Sincerely,

R.N.

Above:
Mr. and Mrs. Walter Hoving at the opening night of the New Opera Company at New York's 44th Street Theatre on October 28, 1942.

Opposite:
Lavish jewelry by Jean Schlumberger. As photographed by Penati for Vogue's September 15, 1970, issue, a model wears a multistrand pearl necklace along with a multistrand lapis lazuli necklace with a diamond and sapphire pendant. The picture is surrounded by a close-up of the lapis lazuli necklace and pendant with canary diamonds, white diamonds, and sapphires set in platinum and eighteen-karat gold.

The day after Nixon's re-election, on November 8, 1972, Henry Platt and the president of Mitsukoshi Department Stores, which was coincidentally celebrating its 300th anniversary, cut the ribbon opening Tiffany's first location in Japan, inside a Mitsukoshi store. Twenty thousand people attended the opening in Tokyo.

In 1974 Platt introduced the work of Elsa Peretti, a young Italian fashion model turned jewelry designer then working in Spain and New York. A genius of the sensual, the simple, the stylish, and the perfect in modern design, she would become the most successful and influential jewelry designer of the twentieth century, probably of all history. Her Peretti open heart would be the unchallenged number-one icon of contemporary jewelry design, and her "Diamonds by the Yard" the greatest boon to the diamond jewelry industry since the six-pronged Tiffany set solitaire diamond ring designed by Charles Lewis Tiffany one hundred years earlier.

Actress, model, and Elsa Schiaparelli's granddaughter Marisa Berenson in Hiro's action cover photograph for Harper's Bazaar, *May 1972. Her Ultrasuede safari jacket by Halston is closed with a faux ivory belt buckle designed by Elsa Peretti, who became Tiffany's star jewelry designer in 1975. Peretti's now-classic sterling silver "Equestrian" belt buckle for Tiffany & Co. can be seen at the lower left.*

The 1974–75 Tiffany Blue Book aptly described her work:

"Sculptured, organic, sensuous, are all words that describe the work of Elsa Peretti, a young jewelry designer with great respect for natural form. What these words do not describe is the simple strength and beauty Miss Peretti achieves with her designs. They are timeless, yet timely; fashionable and at the same time above fashion. They look as handsome when worn as when they are in repose on a flat surface. Finally, they feel as beautiful as they look."

The next year, 1975, Hoving and Platt added yet another name to the roster of Tiffany designers. Angela Cummings's work in mixed metals or in colored stones inlaid in gold (or vice-versa) brought a youthful and lyrical note to Tiffany's design vocabulary.

"Peretti is still Tiffany's darling, but Angela Cummings of Tiffany's is developing," wrote fashion guru and syndicated columnist Eleanor Lambert on December 8, 1979. "A slight, shy young woman who backs away from the limelight, Miss Cummings has nonetheless established a recognizable style of airy, rhythmic designs using unexpected materials like wood, polished crystal and iron with diamonds and other precious stones."

By 1979 the Hoving epoch at Tiffany's was drawing to a close. Van Day Truex, then seventy-five, retired at the beginning of the year, and Hoving put in his place as Tiffany's third design director a thirty-nine-year-old designer, artist, and magazine essayist, John Loring. At the same time Hoving was looking to put Tiffany's into the hands of a younger owner. He had brought the stores' sales to over $70 million a year. He was by then in his early eighties, and it was time to send the grand old dowager of Fifth Avenue on to new and more contemporary adventures in the modern world.

Above:
Cinema star Raquel Welch wore two Tiffany necklaces designed by Sonia Younis when Bill King photographed her for the October 1971 issue of Harper's Bazaar.

Below: An eighteen-karat gold bamboo-motif link bracelet from Tiffany & Co. circa 1970–71. Bamboo has been a popular motif of Tiffany jewelry and table furnishings throughout the twentieth century.

Jean Schlumberger's drawing of a fantastic crested bird makes an exotic background for jewelry. Clockwise from upper right: "Fleurage," a floral garland of multicolored sapphires and diamonds set in platinum and eighteen-karat gold, surrounding "Snowflake," a yellow diamond clip; enamel and eighteen-karat gold "Parrot" brooch with a peridot head, ruby eyes, and coral cheeks; "Fleurage" bracelet; and "Ribbon" diamond earrings. In the center is a Bert Stern photograph of "Oiseau de Paradis" in yellow beryls, rubies, diamonds, amethysts, emeralds, sapphires, and aquamarines, taken for Vogue in 1963.

A Schlumberger necklace modeled by Baroness Thyssen-Bornemisza (née Fiona Campbell-Walter) in Vogue's March 15, 1962, issue. Below is one of Schlumberger's original drawings for the necklace.

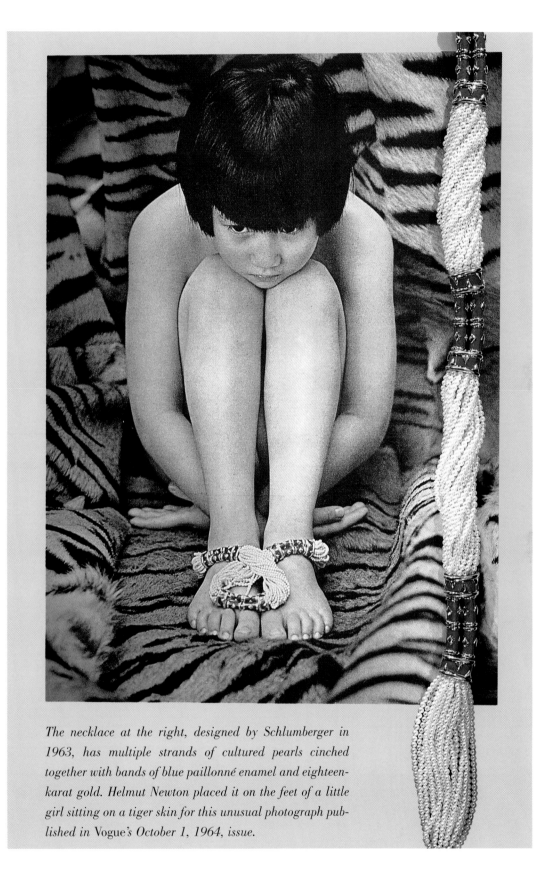

The necklace at the right, designed by Schlumberger in 1963, has multiple strands of cultured pearls cinched together with bands of blue paillonné enamel and eighteen-karat gold. Helmut Newton placed it on the feet of a little girl sitting on a tiger skin for this unusual photograph published in Vogue's *October 1, 1964, issue.*

Opposite:
Jean Schlumberger's "Jasmine" necklace for Tiffany, seen here as photographed by Hiro *for the July 1963 issue of* Harper's Bazaar, *with diamond florets suspended beneath large multicolored sapphires set in platinum and eighteen-karat gold.*

Tiffany has the gift

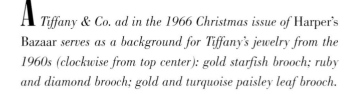

The Tiffar
monds, su
pavé. Plati

iamond Rose: pin with center of brilliant-cut dia
unded by petals, leaves and stem of diamonds
n setting. $ 29,700. including federal tax.   M-2

Tiffany
traditionalism remains
a constant throughout the
years. Pages from Tiffany's 1962 and
1963 Blue Books showing a lavish diamond
spray brooch and "Diamond Rose" pin serve as a
background for Tiffany's 1990s "Victoria"
necklace and bracelet of diamonds set in
platinum, inspired by turn-of-the-
century Tiffany designs.

Tiffany's vividly colored 1960s jewels. Clockwise from top left: In Bill King's 1969 photograph for Harper's Bazaar, *New York City Ballet dancer Linda Merrill wears jewelry designed by Donald Claflin: red rings and a red python skin bracelet with detachable coral and eighteen-karat gold mountings set with diamonds and cabochon emeralds. Multicolored rings and another red python bracelet with a detachable mounting, as photographed by Gene Laurents for* Vogue, *March 1, 1969.*

A pair of fanciful diamond ear clips designed by Jean Schlumberger, as photographed by James Moore for Harper's Bazaar, July 1965. Jerry Salvati's Town & Country, December 1970, photograph of Donald Claflin's brooch, earring, and necklace of yellow sapphires and diamonds set in platinum and eighteen-karat gold.

Opposite: Star model Jean Shrimpton wore Schlumberger's pearl and diamond bracelet and clip when she posed with action-movie star Steve McQueen for Richard Avedon's photograph for Harper's Bazaar, February 1965.

Jewels
of the sea

...tom of page, a green-enamelled dggon stud...
gold veins on diamond wings, diamond t...
Seven wonders of the sea, right—including ...
out on gold chains and wrapped around Princ...
golden waist. The jewelled sea creatures on bot...
ited edition by Donald Claflin of Tiffany. The fi...

Ira ...
jew...
c...

CLIVE LAURENCE

Actress, socialite, and Fiat heiress Princess Ira Fürstenberg daringly wears Donald Claflin's "Dragon" brooches on her bare midriff in this photograph by Penati taken for an article on Tiffany jewelry in the March 1968 issue of Vogue. Tiffany's chairman Walter Hoving wrote Vogue's editor-in-chief Diana Vreeland, "You certainly have discovered a new area on the feminine body where Tiffany jewelry may be worn. I must say I hope it ends there. If it goes much lower, I'm afraid they'll fire me off the Vestry of St. Bartholomew's Church." Center: Four of the pavé diamond and gold Claflin dragon brooches, photographed by Gene Laurents, as they appeared in the Vogue article: from top, one with ruby eyes and tongue; one with sapphire bib and gold arrow tongues; one clutching a pink tourmaline globe and with a gold bell on its tail; and one with green enamel and turquoise studs, perched on a peridot.

Two more Claflin dragon pins appear on this page: at left, one with green enamel scales, a stripe of cabochon rubies, and ruby eyes and tongue; and below, one with a cabochon emerald-studded body and cabochon emerald eye.

Pins of eighteen karat gold by Tiffany designer, Don Berg.
Dagger blades can be removed from their sheaths.   A-56 $
B-56 With diamonds, and turquoise set in coral, $ 3,500.
Designs copyrighted Tiffany & Co., 1970.

56

Jewelry of eighteen karat gold. K. Necklace of sapphires and
yellow and white diamonds with pendant of diamonds set in platinum, $7,500.
Pendant alone (may be worn as a pin), $2,900.
Dagger pins with removable scabbards: L. With diamonds and coral, $3,400.
M. With sapphires, diamonds and green enamel, $2,700.
Designs copyrighted Tiffany & Co., 1970.

TIFFANY & CO.
NEW YORK FIFTH AVENUE AND 57TH STREET
ATLANTA PHIPPS PLAZA · CHICAGO 715 N. MICHIGAN AVE. · HOUSTON GALLERIA POST OAK · SAN FRANCISCO 252 GRANT AVE. · BEVERLY HILLS 9502 WILSHIRE BLVD.

Opposite:
*P**inwheel brooch, a central cluster*
of emeralds with pavé diamond sails,
by Donald Claflin for Tiffany, is
worn by model Alexandra Afganisjew
in Neal Barr's photograph for
Harper's Bazaar, November 1969.

Liza Minnelli, star of Cabaret, New York, New York, *and other Hollywood musicals, has been a fan of Elsa Peretti's jewelry since the mid-1970s. Here she models sterling silver "Bone" cuff bracelets and "Equestrian" belt buckle. Opposite: Minnelli at the Virgin Megastore opening in New York on October 25, 1996, photographed by Marion Curtis. Left: New York Daily News photograph of Minnelli at the same event by Richard Corkery. Below: New York Magazine's 1997 cover photograph of Minnelli by Ruven Afanador.*

Louis Comfort Tiffany & friends on their way to a Costume Ball, Feb. 1913

Above: Gene Moore, who designed the window displays for Tiffany & Co.'s New York store from 1955 to 1995, was acclaimed as the most creative force in his field. The small burglarproof show-windows at Tiffany's posed unique challenges and opportunities for Moore, whose theatrically lit displays were witty, equivocal, often almost Surrealist. At first glance they seemed to be artistic tableaux, yet there was always, except in December Christmas windows, a precious object to remind viewers that Tiffany & Co. was a commercial emporium. Moore's juxtaposition of art and commerce made his displays both ironic and stimulating. Here Moore poses with a display cutout of a classic temple facade and the book he used as his source.

Opposite, top: A Gene Moore window depicts Louis Comfort Tiffany, costumed for his famous Egyptian Fête in 1913, posing for a photographer in front of Tiffany's former building at Thirty-seventh Street and Fifth Avenue.

Opposite, below: Tiffany windows for Christmas by Gene Moore and Jim Henson Productions; right, "Muppet Babies"; left, "Muppet Christmas Carol."

In this Gene Moore–designed display, a holly-wreathed St. Bernard arrives with a bottle of Dom Perignon to save a thirsty Christmas reveller who, though buried in a snowdrift, can still muster the strength to extend her hand-cut crystal champagne glass.

Torn
*Tiffany blue
construction
paper,
cascading tulle,
a hand wearing
an engagement
ring,
Mendelssohn's
"Wedding March,"
and a Tiffany box
with a wedding ring
all combine to create
this memorable
spring bridal season
window display of
1993.*

A jeweled butterfly alighting on a hawser demonstrates
Gene Moore's frequently used visual ploy of contrasting
the raw with the refined.

Right:
A 1978 display shows a block of ice with tongs clasping
a large diamond—a visual pun on gangster argot of the
1930s and 1940s, in which "ice" meant diamonds.

he final two decades of Tiffany's twentieth century began with the arrival of yet another exceptional jewelry designer, Paloma Picasso, the youngest child of the century's greatest artist.

Tiffany's new design director, John Loring, had met Paloma at a luncheon party in Venice given by the legendary art collector Peggy Guggenheim in honor of Paloma's mother, Françoise Gilot. That was in 1966, when Paloma was only sixteen years old. They had remained friends through the intervening years and had often discussed Paloma's first adventures in design, beginning at school in Paris and followed by her professional debuts in Athens with Zolatas and in Paris with Yves Saint Laurent, with whom Loring was also associated at the time. By 1979, the Picasso children had settled their father's more-than-complex estate, and Paloma was ready to continue her career as a designer. Her long friendship with Tiffany & Co.'s new design director led to a not unexpected conclusion. She was presented to Walter Hoving and Henry Platt, by that time Tiffany's president; and, in October of 1980, her first Tiffany jewelry collection was presented to the Tiffany public.

Aggressively chic, uncompromisingly stylized, and high-fashion oriented, Picasso jewelry, while maintaining the Tiffany aesthetic of simple pared-down and tailored forms and unornamented surfaces, went in a different direction from the sensual, organic, and subtly perfected simplicity of Peretti's volumetric forms. Paloma Picasso's signature was to be seen in basic human markings, rather than symbols, in Xs, scribbles, zigzags, and graffiti, all boldly sculpted in gold with flat mirror-polished surface planes. Played off against this was her life-long taste for bright assertive colors, ample forms, and, again, highly polished reflective surfaces that was manifest in massive gold jewels punctuated by lavishly scaled colored gemstones: bright pink tourmalines, brighter-still orange fire opals, chrome green tourmalines, acid blue zircons, or clear, sky-blue aquamarines.

The success of such colorful brashness would have delighted Louis Comfort Tiffany. It would continue to delight the public and press throughout the remainder of the century.

In 1980 work was also begun on a new look in Tiffany watches to embody the same simplicity of form, composition, and surface that Tiffany design had set as its goal since the arrival of Van Day Truex— a look that would move totally away from the pervasive influence of the late-eighteenth-century designs of Louis Breguet, which had set the standard for watch design for nearly two centuries. The result was the Tiffany "Atlas" watch, first presented in 1982. The success of Tiffany's tailored, pared-down, definitively American watch line was so immediate that "Atlas" clocks and then "Atlas" writing instruments were soon added to the collection. "Atlas" jewelry would be added in 1995 to complete a design statement that intentionally looked into the twenty-first century.

In 1981, Walter Hoving retired from Tiffany & Co., concluding an always remarkable over-half-century career as a great leader of American merchandising, marketing, and retailing. Henry Platt succeeded him for a period as Tiffany's chairman, but the company's ownership had been in flux since Hoving's decision to sell in 1979. A new ownership team led by William R. Chaney, the former president of the Avon Corporation and a member of Tiffany's board of directors since 1980, would take over Tiffany & Co. in 1984 with Chaney as its new chairman and chief executive officer. Thereafter, the 1980s and 1990s can legitimately be called the Chaney Years.

Tiffany's competitive advantage through superior product design and superior quality in materials and craftsmanship would remain a constant throughout the Chaney decades, just as it had remained a constant throughout the Hoving epoch. Times had changed both socially and economically, however, and the old tried-and-true Hoving retailing

Above:
Three Paloma Picasso jeweled gold cuff bracelets with, from top, a green tourmaline zigzag; a diamond and aquamarine quarter-circle; and three hexagonal palm citrines.

Preceding pages:
Page 194, top: Selections from Tiffany's "Atlas" collection, 1995. Left, eighteen-karat gold strap watch, bracelets, and rings set with diamonds and sapphires. Right, eighteen-karat gold bracelets and rings set with diamonds and rubies.

Page 195: Three 1996 "Fireworks" brooches with multicolored gemstones from Tiffany & Co. light up the sky over Manhattan. The background illustration is by Joe Eula, who also illustrated the ever-popular manual on etiquette, Tiffany's Table Manners for Teenagers, written in 1961 by Walter Hoving, Tiffany's chairman.

Above:
Tiffany jewelry designer Paloma Picasso, as photographed by Walter Chin in 1995, wears her signature "Scribble," "Little Secrets X," "Heart," and "Love and Kisses" pins.
Left and right: Paloma Picasso photographed by Robert Mapplethorpe for a double page advertisement in the October 1980 issue of Interview *magazine announcing her first jewelry collection for Tiffany's.*

philosophy of continual inventory improvement targeted at a relatively small but loyal customer base had become unrealistic. The world market had grown, and broader merchandise offerings targeted at a broader audience was the only direction that could lead to significant growth and to the financial progress needed to enhance Tiffany's place in the ever more ferociously competitive luxury goods retail environment, by then filled with international players. Chaney took that direction and began a brilliantly successful program of rapid international as well as domestic expansion.

New merchandise categories emerged. The Tiffany silver jewelry department received considerable design and merchandising attention to reach a younger audience and grew to be the world's largest fine sterling silver jewelry business. Leather goods and accessories, discontinued by Hoving in the late 1950s, were reinstated in the early 1980s, this time including Tiffany silk scarves and Tiffany neckties in addition to the traditional handbags; Tiffany fragrances were introduced in 1987. Elsa Peretti's design collection was expanded in the early 1980s to include table furnishings in china, crystal, and silver; and other name designers were invited to design tablewares exclusively for Tiffany & Co. These include the greatest living master of Venetian glassmaking, Archimede Seguso, and Ireland's great doyenne of design and "living national treasure," Sybil Connolly.

Tiffany's returned to Europe; first with a European flagship store in London's Old Bond Street, followed by stores in Zurich's Bahnhofstrasse, Milan's via Montenapoleone, and Munich's Residenzstrasse. New Tiffany locations also opened in the Asian-Pacific region in Singapore, Hong Kong, Taipei, Sydney, and in 1996 an important flagship store on Tokyo's Ginza.

Before the close of the century, there would be over 120 Tiffany & Co. stores in over 40 countries worldwide. Daily Tiffany sales would average

Above: The classic fragrances of Tiffany & Co.: "Tiffany," "Tiffany for Men," and "Trueste." The "Tiffany" fragrance bottle echoes the clean architectural lines of Tiffany's streamlined New York headquarters store on Fifth Avenue and Fifty-seventh Street.

Below: Marina Schiano's 1997 portrait of Franca Sossana, editor-in-chief of Vogue Italia, *at her Milan home wearing two brooches from Tiffany's "Fireworks" collection on her Romeo Gigli skirt.*

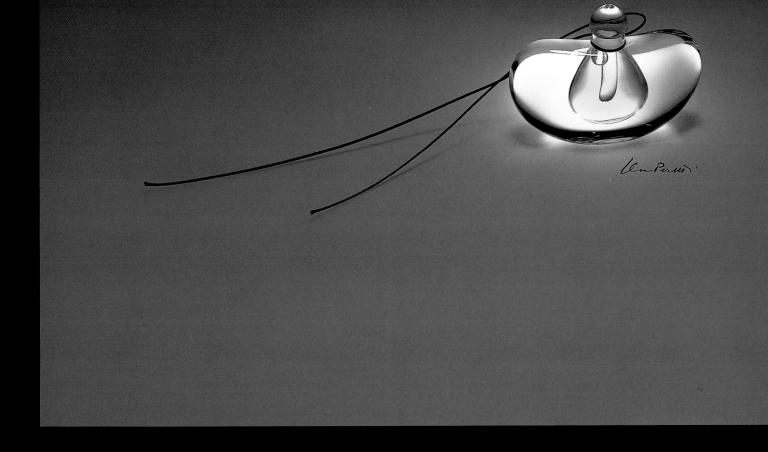

The critic Nancy Hall-Duncan wrote that Hiro could transform objects into "monumental icons having uncanny presence, scale and importance" (Contemporary Photographers, New York: St. James Press, 1995, p. 489). The magic of Hiro's photography is nowhere better exemplified than in his haunting image of Elsa Peretti's hand-carved rock crystal bottle for the fragrance she created for Tiffany & Co. in 1981.

Angela Cummings designed jewelry for Tiffany from 1967 to 1983, drawing her inspiration from nature and using materials such as copper, steel, wood, and hematite in addition to gold, silver, and colored gems. Her 1981 leaf necklace of eighteen-karat gold and copper surrounds a photograph of a Tiffany Christmas table setting with a diamond necklace designed by Cummings in 1980.

H.M. Queen Eliza-
beth II at the Guards
Polo Club in 1996
presenting a gift
from Tiffany & Co.
–London in the
famous blue box.

Diana, Princess of
Wales, at Wimbledon
on July 2, 1994,
wearing a Tiffany
"Signature II"
eighteen-karat gold
bracelet and earrings.

In Bill Cunningham's photo-
graph (below), Jacqueline
Kennedy Onassis, who edit-
ed a series of six Tiffany &
Co. books, holds a copy of
the first in the series, The
New Tiffany Table Settings,
in front of Tiffany & Co.'s
New York headquarters on
October 23, 1981.

Jacqueline Kennedy
Onassis in 1992(above)
wearing her favorite
Jean Schlumberger
eighteen-karat gold
and white enamel
"Banana" earrings.

well over $3 million a day, a handsome improvement over the $4.98 taken in by the twenty-five-year-old Charles Lewis Tiffany on his first day of business in September 1837.

With such distinctive collections as the streamlined stainless steel watches and accessories of the "Streamerica" collection and the lavishly jeweled starbursts of "Fireworks," both inspired by Tiffany's designs for the 1939 New York World's Fair; its "Atlas" collection, with its witty, suave, and stylish play on the digitalization of the universe by the Information Age; and its Tiffany "Nature" collection, reaffirming Tiffany's and America's age-old tenet that "Mother Nature is the best designer," Tiffany & Co. galloped ahead to stand out in the Age of Brand Names and the Age of Uniformity that end the twentieth century.

At the beginning of the century, Tiffany & Co's first design director, Louis Comfort Tiffany, said quite prophetically, "We are going after the money there is in art, but the art is there all the same."

One hundred years later, Tiffany's still stands by his words, as it does by those of his father and Tiffany's founder, Charles Lewis Tiffany, who stated the case and the key to Tiffany's worldwide success more gracefully:

"Good Design Is Good Business."

John Loring
February 1997

Right:
The most extravagant diamond brooch made by Tiffany & Co. in the twentieth century had a canary diamond weighing 107 carats crowned by a 23-carat D-flawless pear-shaped diamond and surrounded by an additional 80 carats of fine white marquise and pear-shaped diamonds. Designed by Maurice Galli and John Loring in 1988, it was priced at $15,000,000.

Elsa Peretti's jewelry for Tiffany & Co. is an outstanding achievement of twentieth-century design. Her sensual, sculptural forms drawn from nature are masterpieces of organic abstraction. Above: The dynamic Peretti in a moment of reverie, photographed by Bill King for Harper's Bazaar, October 1980; she is wearing a hexagonal stainless steel and diamond ring, an eighteen-karat gold mesh scarf, gold and diamond stud earrings, and highly important gold and diamond cuff links, all of her design.

Opposite: This image of Peretti's classic "Bone" silver cuff bracelet, as photographed by Hiro in 1984, is one of the century's most memorable photographs of jewelry.

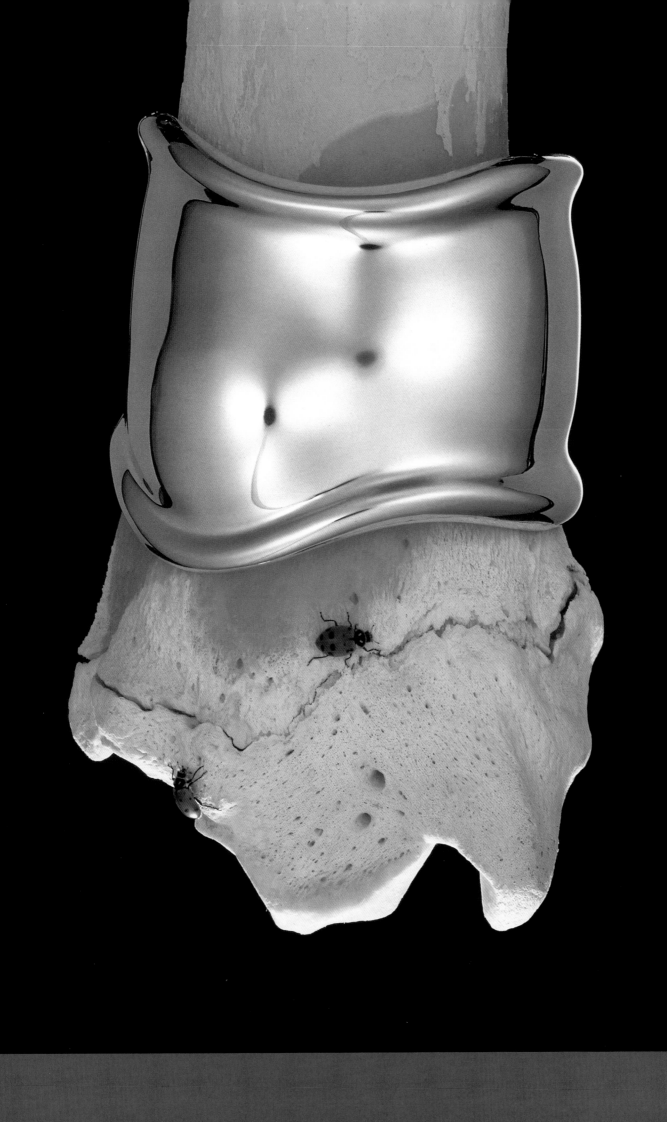

Elsa Peretti's designs for the home made exclusively for Tiffany & Co. Opposite: Sterling silver "Bone" candlestick and footed Venetian glass fishbowl with a piranha biting a model's fingernail, photographed by Hiro, 1984.
Above: Sterling silver flask pendant, the first piece of jewelry Peretti designed, photographed with an orchid and a praying mantis by Hiro, 1988.

In these early 1990s photographs, Hiro's ongoing fascination with water accentuates the sensuality of Elsa Peretti's lacquer bracelets (above) and "Diamonds by the Yard" (right), round-cut diamonds on eighteen-karat gold chains, first sold by Tiffany & Co. in lengths specified by its clients.

Opposite: Hiro's surrealistic photograph of water leaping with a gravity-defying will of its own from Peretti's sterling silver pitcher with a vermeil lining, 1996.

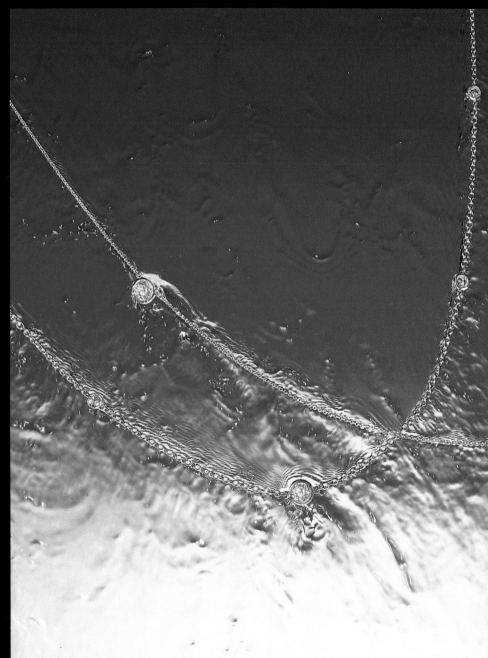

Preceding pages:
These photographs, all taken by Victor Skrebneski for Town & Country, show his genius for capturing the compelling juxtaposition of precious jewels and beautiful skin. Left: In this mannered study of diamonds and feminine allure, published in Town & Country in August 1983, the painterly pink markings on a sheet of paper held across the model's shoulder as well as her multicolored, pearlescent nails serve as foils for the drama of highly important pear-shaped diamonds from the 1983 "Diamonds of Tiffany" collection.

Top right: Line necklaces and bracelets of square-cut diamonds and a ring set with an 11.90-carat "starburst" diamond modeled by Kim Charlton. In a witty gesture of throwaway opulence, an important 26.54-carat emerald-cut diamond dangles from her line necklaces set with a total of 395 diamonds; this photograph appeared in Town & Country in August 1984.

Below right: Skrebneski's seductive photograph of supermodel Cindy Crawford wearing a Claude Montana swimsuit and jewelry by Paloma Picasso: an eighteen-karat gold and moonstone ring, a hexagonal palm citrine ring, and a cultured pearl and aquamarine bead choker with an eighteen-karat gold and calibré diamond ball clasp. On the wrist of model Tara Shannon are Paloma Picasso's "Graffiti" and "Heart" bracelets. The photograph appeared in Town & Country in February 1985.

Above and opposite:
Skrebneski's studies of moody and richly adorned beauty for Town & Country. In the photograph above from the February 1990 issue, the model on the left wears Tiffany's three-strand cultured pearl necklace with a 100-carat tanzanite set in diamonds, a matching ring, and ear clips; and on the right, a Tiffany multistrand cultured pearl necklace with a diamond ribbon cross set with a large Burmese pearl, matching ear clips, and ring. Opposite: Important sapphire and diamond necklace with matching ear clips, Town & Country, February 1983.

A necklace of 28 oval rubies and 212 marquise diamonds shown with a second necklace of rubies and diamonds, diamond bracelets, earrings, and solitaire ring. For the February 1988 Town & Country Skrebneski photographed Deborah Harris posing against a photographic reproduction of Amedeo Modigliani's Le Grand Nu of 1919 and wearing this arresting collection of Tiffany jewels.

Above:

Paloma Picasso's moonstone "Lightning" bracelet (now in Chicago's Field Museum) and matching ring, photographed by Skrebneski for Town & Country's February 1984 issue; the bracelet's huge moonstone holds its own against Claude Montana's magenta leather head-dress, worn by Kim Charlton, who is also wearing a Paloma Picasso eighteen-karat gold and diamond "dog collar" choker.

Opposite:

Paloma Picasso wearing her "Lightning" moonstone bracelet, cabochon rubelite ring, and chain hoop earrings, photographed by Bill King in 1985.

Opposite:

Kenro Izu's portrait of Paloma Picasso wearing her most important jewel, a diamond ribbon "X's" necklace, as well as earrings set with exceptional colored gemstones, including tanzanites, tourmalines, peridots, and aquamarines. The necklace was designed for Tiffany's 150th anniversary, celebrated in 1987.

Above and right:
Paloma Picasso jewelry shown in photographs by Skrebneski for Town & Country, February 1991. Right: Diamond ribbon and morganite necklace worn with a plain diamond ribbon necklace and pink tourmaline and diamond drop earrings. (When pink beryl was discovered, the American Museum of Natural History named it "morganite" in honor of the great American capitalist J. Pierpont Morgan, a major benefactor of the museum.) Above: Nastassia, at left, wears a blue zircon ring, aquamarine earrings, and a morganite necklace augmented with an aquamarine brooch and a green tourmaline brooch; Jeannette wears a gold and diamond necklace with an aquamarine pendant, a matching ring, and pavé diamond "X" earrings.

Opposite:
Skrebneski experiments with striking contrasts, here creating a "tribal" setting for a gold mesh chain and pavé diamond "egg" that is more regal than tribal. The incredibly intricate goldwork, known as the chaine à l'impératrice, was originally conceived in Paris (where this example was made for Tiffany's) for the beautiful Empress Eugènie, wife of Napoleon III. Art critic John Canaday, who wrote the essay "The Artful Body" that accompanied this picture for Town & Country's May 1982 issue, said that this photograph depicted "Primitive woman, dressed as she might have been before the dawn of history, in patterns of colored clays."

Right: Daughters of twentieth-century icons Ingrid Bergman and Pablo Picasso are juxtaposed in Eric Boman's 1988 photograph of Isabella Rossellini wearing a bracelet and rings set with amethysts and tourmalines by Paloma Picasso for Tiffany & Co. *Below:* The German magazine Madame featured Paloma Picasso's amethyst and diamond jewelry in this 1995 abstract photographic composition by Raoul Manuel Schnell.

Below:

These sterling silver pitchers from Tiffany's 1995 "American Classics" collection are based on the distinctively American and fluidly sculptural, spiral, and wrapped forms of 1930s Ohio Art Deco ceramics.

Right:

Tiffany's "American Garden" sterling silver flatware, introduced in 1992 and based on Tiffany Arts and Crafts designs; each piece shows a different American flower, fruit, grain, or vegetable, reflecting Tiffany's ongoing celebration of American nature. Its asymmetrical patterns echo Tiffany's great Japanesque flatware pattern "Audubon," introduced in 1871 and still a bestseller almost 130 years later. Pieces of Tiffany's "American Garden" porcelain can be seen in the background.

In the course of his long career, the master Venetian glassmaker Archimede Seguso has worked in radically different styles, yet all his pieces are elegant and flawlessly executed. Tiffany's began its association with Seguso (seen left center in his Murano studio in 1988) in the mid-1950s, and their association continues to this day. In the early 1950s Seguso revived the eighteenth-century Venetian "merletto" glass, in which fine translucent lines form lacelike patterns, but he used the technique to achieve his own emphatically twentieth-century objectives. His volumetric and fluidly asymmetrical work is inspired by sunlight on the water of Venice, and Manfredi Bellati photographed several 1990s Seguso pieces, designed and made exclusively for Tiffany's, with their source of inspiration.

"Tiffany Nature," a 1996 jewelry collection based on traditional Tiffany designs by Paulding Farnham and Donald Claflin and created under the aegis of Jeanne Daniel, Tiffany's executive vice-president of merchandising, are placed here upon background images of nature. Opposite, from left: Diamond dragonfly pin, pavé diamond frog pin with cabochon emerald eyes, and pearl and diamond dragonfly on a pearl and platinum chain.

Above: Jumping pavé diamond frog pin, three-strand cultured pearl necklace ornamented with a pavé diamond turtle, and a pavé frog pendant holding a black Tahitian pearl. Right: Pavé diamond and platinum crab holding a large black Tahitian pearl.

Tiffany's "Atlas" collection, introduced in 1995, was a development of its Atlas wristwatch designed in 1980 by Tiffany's design director John Loring and based on the clock held by the figure of Atlas, the signature fixture over the entrance of all Tiffany's headquarters since 1853. The style of the Atlas watch is classically modern, with perfect flatness, chaste simplicity, and bold, brightly polished Roman numerals in relief contrasting with a matte gold background. Above: An eighteen-karat gold Atlas watch sits atop a page of original sketches for Atlas jewelry by John Loring dated April 30, 1994. Right: Heather Stewart Whyte models the Atlas watch and earrings in a photograph by Mikael Jansson for a Tiffany & Co. advertisement.

K*nife-edged, crisp double bands, and Roman numerals with contrasting matte and polished surfaces characterize Tiffany's Atlas bracelets and rings, all in eighteen-karat gold, or with round diamonds, calibrated sapphires, or rubies.*

Above:

Gifts for men from Tiffany's "Atlas" collection: sterling silver watch, letter opener, belt buckle, money clip, and black resin fountain pen with gold-filled detailing. The ribbing evokes the fluting on classical columns.

Right:

This Tiffany "Allures" inlaid stone jewelry with nautical themes was designed by John Loring in the early 1990s. A striped lapis lazuli, mother-of-pearl, and gold seahorse; gold sailboat bangle bracelet; pin with striped sail; and a striped sail earring are shown on a background of a 1930s Tiffany Blue Book page with nautical themes.

Tiffany's introduced its "Streamerica" collection of watches and accessories in 1990 to celebrate the fiftieth anniversary of its New York headquarters store. Evoking the aerodynamic principles of the 1939 New York World's Fair "streamlining," the Streamerica collection evolved from the profile of a DC-3 wing and the bolted metal sheeting of airplane construction. It pays homage to stainless steel, the great twentieth-century material that Tiffany & Co. pioneered with the stainless steel showcases designed for its 1905 store at Thirty-seventh Street and Fifth Avenue by Stanford White. Above: "Streamerica" inkwell, picture frame, and letter opener. Opposite: "Streamerica" watch, key ring, and three paperweight boxes.

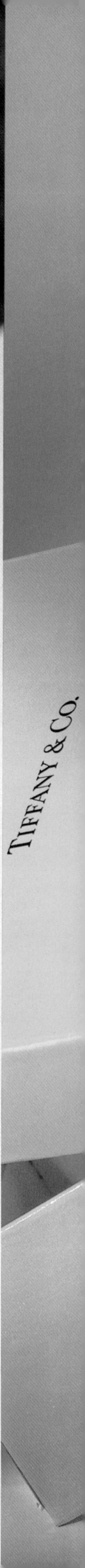

The hope
and dream of
many young
women—
a classic
Tiffany & Co.
ad used from
1994.

TIFFANY & CO.

*F*our multicolored faceted
gemstone brooches from
Tiffany's 1993 "Fireworks"
collection.

Tiffany's 1990s "Etoile" jewelry collection, modeled by Heather Stewart Whyte, features earrings and bracelets of eighteen-karat gold star-studded with diamonds.

Right: A photograph by Kenro Izu of an amethyst, tsavorite, and diamond brooch from Tiffany's recent "Fireworks" collection, seen against a background of a New York harbor fireworks display.

Above: "Etoile" solitaire diamond ring and "Etoile" wedding band.

Credits

Collages conceived and created by John Loring.

The photographs on the following pages were taken by Billy Cunningham:
Pages 33, 35–37, 54 (top and center), 58–60, 61 (top), 62, 64–69, 79, 80 (top left), 81, 88 (bracelet), 89–90, 102, 104–5 (left and right bottom), 110, 114–15, 124 (top), 128–29, 130, 131 (upper right), 132, 138–39, 141–43, 146, 150–51, 155, 167, 171 (bottom), 176, 195, 200 (center), 225, 229.

The collage overlays listed on the following pages were photographed for this book by Billy Cunningham (see also additional photo and collection credits below for objects and/or photographs within collages): Pages 5, 13, 14–15 (top), 18–19, 22–23, 28–31, 39, 41, 46–47, 48–49 (center), 50, 55, 70, 72 (inset upper left), 76, 77 (pin top left), 83, 86–87 (collages at upper left and center), 93, 95, 97 (top right), 100 (rings), 101 (upper left and lower right), 106 (top), 109, 111–13, 117, 121, 122–23, 127, 134 (bracelets), 135, 136 (above center), 140, 147, 148 (brooch), 149 (top), 157, 159 (jewels), 163, 172–73, 175 (necklace), 178–79, 185, 224, 240.

Additional photo and collection credits:

Page 1: Photo, Craig Cutler.

Page 2: Photo by Edward Steichen, Courtesy *Vogue*. Copyright © 1940 (renewed 1968) by The Condé Nast Publications Inc.

Page 5: Background photo, Corbis-Bettman; necklace, The Sataloff Family and the Cluchey Children.

Page 6: Photo, Jesse Gerstein; Collection of Richard McGeehan.

Page 8: All photos Mary Hilliard except bottom center, Janet C. Koltick, Globe Photos, Inc. Copyright © 1994.

Pages 10–11: Photo, Tiffany & Co. Archives.

Page 13: Background drawing and photo, Tiffany & Co. Archives; necklace, Tiffany & Co.

Pages 14–15: Below, Tiffany & Co. Archives; top, backgrounds Corbis-Bettman; stereo photos, private collection; necklace, private collection.

Page 17: Brooch, Tiffany & Co. Archives; drawing, Edimedia, Paris.

Pages 18–19: Background photo, © LL-Viollet, Paris; drawings, Tiffany & Co. Archives; stereo photo, private collection; brooch, James Robinson, Inc., N.Y.

Page 21: Top, Virginia Museum of Fine Arts, Richmond; The Sydney and Frances Lewis Art Nouveau Fund; photo Katherine Wetzel © 1985; below, High Museum of Art, Atlanta; Virginia Carroll Crawford Collection, 1984.170.

Pages 22–23: Center below, background photo, Corbis-Bettman; drawing and brooch, Tiffany & Co. Archives.

Page 23: Above, background photo, Corbis-Bettman; bow brooch and heart pendant, Fred Leighton, N.Y.; bow brooch with watch pendant, private collection; cigarette case, Tiffany & Co. Archives; below, chrysanthemum brooch, Christie's Images.

Page 24: Toilet set, Sotheby's; drawing, Tiffany & Co. Archives.

Page 27: Photos, Tiffany & Co. Archives.

Pages 28–29: Drawing and background photo, Tiffany & Co. Archives; all jewelry, The Sataloff Family and the Cluchey Children.

Pages 30–31: Background photos, Tiffany & Co. Archives; bracelets, The Sataloff Family and the Cluchey Children.

Page 32: Photo, Tiffany & Co. Archives.

Page 33: Jewelry, Tiffany & Co. Archives, except brooch at center left and jewel casket, Lillian Nassau Ltd., N.Y.

Page 34: Above, Collection of the Hispanic Society of America, N.Y.; below, photo, Corbis-Bettman.

Page 35: Vases and tiles, Lillian Nassau Ltd., N.Y.

Page 36: Cup, private collection, N.Y.; tiles, private collection.

Page 37: Vase, Courtesy Lillian Nassau Ltd., N.Y., Collection Louis C. Tiffany Museum, Nagoya, Japan; tiles, Courtesy Lillian Nassau Ltd., N.Y., private collection.

Page 38: Top, drawings, Tiffany & Co. Archives; below, brooch and drawing, Walters Art Gallery, Baltimore.

Page 39: Drawing, Walters Art Gallery, Baltimore; Gift of Tiffany & Co.; background photos, Tiffany & Co. Archives; brooch at right: Primavera Gallery, N.Y.; brooch at left, Fred Leighton, N.Y.

Page 40: Vase, The Metropolitan Museum of Art, N.Y., Gift of Edward D. Adams, 1904.

Page 41: Photo inset at upper left: Tiffany & Co. Archives; background photo: © LL-Viollet, Paris; brooch, Tiffany & Co. Archives.

Pages 42–43: Background photo: UPI/Corbis-Bettman; silver dish, photo, Christie's, N.Y.

Page 44: Photo, Art and Architecture Collection, Miriam and Ira D. Wallach Division of Art, Prints and Photographs, The New York Public Library, Astor, Lenox and Tilden Foundations.

Page 45: Photo and drawing, Tiffany & Co. Archives.

Pages 46–47: All background drawings and photos, Tiffany & Co. Archives; "Fire" opals, Tiffany & Co.; brooch, lower right, page 47, The Sataloff Family and the Cluchey Children.

Page 48: Silver bowl at upper left, private collection; photo, Tom Jenkins; photo at lower left, Tiffany & Co. Archives.

Pages 48–49: Background photo © LL-Viollet, Paris; "Navajoe" vase on lower left, Collection of Gloria Manney; "Aztec" bowl on lower right, private collection.

Pages 50–51: Bow brooch, Collection Neil Lane, L.A.; necklace, photo Sotheby's; background photo, Tiffany & Co. Archives.

Pages 52–53: Photo at upper left, from *L'Exposition Internationale des Arts Décoratifs Modernes A Turin 1902* (Darmstadt: Alexander Koch, 1902); coffee service, Collection of the Newark Museum; Purchase 1986 The Members Fund; photo, Jesse Gerstein.

Page 54: Top, all objects and drawing, Lillian Nassau Ltd., N.Y.; center, drawings, Tiffany & Co. Archives; clock, Tiffany & Co.; clock at bottom, Collection of Carl Heck, Aspen, Colorado; photo, Sotheby's.

Page 55: Pencils and background photo, MetLife Archives.

Page 56: Photo, Christie's, N.Y.

Page 57: Top photo, Tiffany & Co. Archives; bottom photo, UPI/Corbis-Bettman.

Page 58: Tiles and scarabs, Lillian Nassau Ltd., N.Y.; scarab necklace, Collection Louis C. Tiffany Museum, Nagoya, Japan.

Page 59: Necklaces, Tiffany & Co. Archives; plaque, Lillian Nassau Ltd., N.Y.

Page 60: Enamel box at upper left, private collection; all other objects and book, Lillian Nassau Ltd., N.Y.

Page 61 (top): Two vases at left, Collection Louis C. Tiffany Museum, Nagoya, Japan; crate, plaque, and vase at right, Lillian Nassau Ltd., N.Y.

Page 61 (below): Collection Louis C. Tiffany Museum, Nagoya, Japan; photo, Christie's Images.

Page 62: Necklaces, Tiffany & Co. Archives; mosaic, Lillian Nassau Ltd., N.Y.

Page 63: Charles Hosmer Morse Museum of American Art, Winter Park, Fla.

Pages 64–65: Lillian Nassau Ltd., N.Y.

Page 66: Background panels, Lillian Nassau Ltd., N.Y.; ceramic and crystal vases, Tiffany & Co. Archives; silver vases, Tiffany & Co.

Page 67: Box and vase, Lillian Nassau Ltd., N.Y.; candlestick at left, Tiffany & Co.; candlestick at right, Tiffany & Co. Archives.

Page 68: Bronze, Lillian Nassau Ltd., N.Y.; necklace, Tiffany & Co. Archives.

Page 69: Jewelry, Tiffany & Co. Archives; tiles, Lillian Nassau Ltd., N.Y.

Page 70: Brooch at top, private collection; brooch at bottom, background photo, and drawing, Tiffany & Co. Archives.

Page 71: Necklace, The Metropolitan Museum of Art, N.Y., Gift of Sarah E. Hanley, 1946, 46.168.1; photo at upper right, Tiffany & Co. Archives.

Pages 72–73: Bowl at upper left, private collection; box at upper right, Charles Hosmer Morse Museum of American Art, Winter Park, Fla.; screen at lower right, Collection Louis C. Tiffany Museum, Nagoya, Japan; background photos, UPI/Corbis-Bettman.

Pages 74–75: Postcards, Courtesy of the California Historical Society, San Francisco, Ephemera Collection; cup at left, The Walters Art Gallery, Baltimore; urn at right, Allentown Art Museum, Gift of Bethlehem Steel Corp. 1985.25.

Page 76: Photo at bottom center, Underwood & Underwood/Corbis-Bettman; all other background drawings and military photos, Tiffany & Co. Archives.

Page 77: Background photos at upper left, Corbis-Bettman; photo at upper right, Reprinted with the permission of Simon & Schuster from *Rickenbacker: An Autobiography* by Edward V. Rickenbacker; Copyright © 1967 by Edward V. Rickenbacker; "Wings" pin, Collection George Bianchetti; medal at bottom, Courtesy of United States Naval Academy Museum.

Page 78: Drawings, Tiffany & Co. Archives.

Page 79: Bow brooches, clockwise from upper left, Primavera Gallery, N.Y.; Tiffany & Co.; Tiffany & Co.; James Robinson, Inc., N.Y.; Tiffany & Co.; background drawings, Tiffany & Co. Archives.

Page 80: Left, background drawing, Tiffany & Co. Archives; bar pin at top, Stephen-Russell, N.Y.; bracelet, ring, and jabot pin, Collection Neil Lane, L.A.; watch at right, photo Sotheby's.

Page 81: Left, background drawing, Tiffany & Co. Archives; dimes, private collection; bracelet, Collection Neil Lane, L.A.

Page 82: Lipton cup, Collection Glasgow Museum and Art Galleries, Glasgow, Scotland; top photo, Kevin Logan; bottom photo, UPI/Corbis-Bettman.

Page 83: Background drawings, © 1933 R.H. Donnelley, A company of the Dun & Bradstreet Corporation, Reproduced by Permission; coffee service photo, Tiffany & Co. Archives; center photo, Kaufmann & Fabry Co.; ticket, private collection.

Pages 84–85: Bottom photo, Man Ray, © 1997 Artists Rights Society (ARS), New York/ADAGP/Man Ray Trust, Paris. Originally appeared in *Harper's Bazaar* (December 1936). All other photos, top left and right, Tiffany & Co. Archives.

Pages 86–87: Background photos, clockwise from upper left: UPI/Corbis-Bettman; The Bettman Archives; UPI/Corbis-Bettman; Lyndhurst, A property of the National Trust for Historical Preservation; UPI/Corbis-Bettman; UPI/Bettman News photos; *Harper's Bazaar* (November 1936, p. 111); *Harper's Bazaar* (April 1938). Jewelry, clockwise from upper left: brooch, James Robinson, Inc., N.Y.; necklace with pendant, Sotheby's; bar brooch and pearl brooch, Tiffany & Co. Archives; watches, Stephen-Russell, N.Y.; emerald brooch, Macklowe Gallery, N.Y.; drawings, Tiffany & Co. Archives.

Page 88: Hoyningen-Huene photo, Courtesy Staley-Wise Gallery, N.Y.; bracelet, Collection Neil Lane, L.A.

Page 89: Collage, Courtesy *Vogue*. Copyright © 1934 (renewed 1962) by The Condé Nast Publications Inc.; jewelry, Collection Neil Lane, L.A.

Page 90: Pearls, Tiffany & Co.

Page 91: Bracelet, Christie's Images; Steichen photo, Courtesy *Vogue*. Copyright © 1934 (renewed 1962) by The Condé Nast Publications Inc.

Page 92: Poster at top, Courtesy Posters Please Inc., N.Y.; Steichen photos, Courtesy *Vogue*. Copyright © 1939 (renewed 1967) by The Condé Nast Publications Inc.; overlay drawings of necklaces and earrings, Maurice Galli, Tiffany & Co.

Page 93: Background photo, Dmitri Kessel, *Life Magazine*, © Time Inc.; necklace, Tiffany & Co. Archives.

Page 94: Hoyningen-Huene photo, Courtesy Staley-Wise Gallery, N.Y.; bracelet at left, photo Tiffany & Co. Archives; bracelet at right, private collection.

Page 95 (top): Courtesy *Vogue*. Copyright © 1936 (renewed 1964) by The Condé Nast Publications Inc.; cosmetic set, Tiffany & Co. Archives; vanity case, John P. Axelrod Collection, Courtesy Museum of Fine Arts, Boston.

Page 95 (bottom): Louise Dahl-Wolfe photo, Courtesy Staley-Wise Gallery, N.Y.; bracelet at left, Stephen-Russell, N.Y.; bracelet at right, Collection Neil Lane, L.A.

Page 96: Both photos, Courtesy *Vogue*. Copyright 1934 (renewed 1962) by The Condé Nast Publications Inc.; all bracelets, Sotheby's.

Page 97: Photo at top, © 1997 Artists Rights Society (ARS), New York/ADAGP/Man Ray Trust, Paris; photo at bottom, Courtesy *Vogue*. Copyright © 1936 (renewed 1969) by The Condé Nast Publications Inc.

Page 98: Courtesy *Vogue*. Copyright © 1937 (renewed 1965) by The Condé Nast Publications Inc.

Page 99: Courtesy *Vogue*. Copyright © 1939 (renewed 1967) by The Condé Nast Publications Inc.

Page 100 (top): Courtesy *Vogue*. Copyright © 1940 (renewed 1968) by The Condé Nast Publications Inc.

Page 100 (bottom): Courtesy *Vogue*. Copyright © 1936 (renewed 1964) by The Condé Nast Publications Inc.; ring at right, private collection; ring at left, Macklowe Gallery, N.Y.

Page 101 (top left and right): Courtesy *Vogue*. Copyright © 1937 (renewed 1965) by The Condé Nast Publications Inc.; bracelet at upper left, Tiffany & Co. Archives.

Page 101 (bottom): Courtesy *Vogue*. Copyright © 1938 (renewed 1966) by The Condé Nast Publications Inc.; bracelets, Fred Leighton, N.Y.

Page 102: Clock, private collection; horses, private collection.

Page 103: Clock, Christie's Images.

Pages 104–5: Photo at top center, Tiffany & Co. Archives.

Page 106: Cocktail set and drawing, Tiffany & Co.; tea set, Collection Norwest Corporation, Minneapolis.

Page 107: Centerpiece and candelabra at top left, Christie's, N.Y.; background photo, Tiffany & Co. Archives; drawing at lower right, Tiffany & Co. Design Department.

Page 108: Louise Dahl-Wolfe photo, Courtesy Staley-Wise Gallery, N.Y.; bracelet, Christie's Images.

Page 109: Hoyningen-Huene photo, Courtesy Staley-Wise Gallery, N.Y.; two bracelets at top and earrings, Stephen-Russell, N.Y.; bottom bracelet, private collection.

Page 110: Background drawings, Tiffany & Co. Archives; drawing of emerald tiara, Maurice Galli, Tiffany & Co.

Page 111: Background photo, Anton Bruehl, Courtesy Vogue. Copyright © 1939 (renewed 1967) by The Condé Nast Publications Inc.; drawings, Tiffany & Co. Archives.

Pages 112–13: Top left, background, Curt Teich Postcard Archives/Lake County Museum, Ill.; top center, background, Courtesy Posters Please Inc., N.Y.; background photo, center, Tiffany & Co. Archives; drawings of jewelry, Maurice Galli, Tiffany & Co.; top right and bottom right, background photos, UPI/Corbis-Bettman.

Pages 114–15: Background, © The Grinnell Litho. Co., N.Y.; drawings, Tiffany & Co. Archives.

Page 116: Photos, Elliott Kaufman.

Page 117: Background photo, Ronny Jaques for Town & Country (April 1954, p. 56); drawing, Maurice Galli, Tiffany & Co.

Page 119: Tiffany & Co. Archives.

Page 121: Background photos, UPI/Corbis-Bettman; clippings, The New York Times; drawing, Tiffany & Co. Archives.

Pages 122–23: Backgrounds, Tiffany & Co. Archives; pin, Collection Neil Lane, L.A.

Page 124: Emlen Etting drawing, Courtesy Stubbs Books & Prints, Inc.; bracelet, Stephen-Russell, N.Y.; catalogue page at bottom, Tiffany & Co. Archives.

Page 125: Top, Christie's, N.Y.; bottom, Town & Country (April 1954) and The Saturday Evening Post (January 31, 1953).

Page 126 (from top): The National Gem Collection, Smithsonian Institution, Washington, D.C.; Tiffany & Co. Archives; Ivan Dmitri, Used with permission from the The Saturday Evening Post © 1953.

Page 127: Photo by Virginia Thoren for Town & Country (July 1956).

Pages 128–29: Drawing, Marcel Vertès, from Harper's Bazaar (September 15, 1940); bracelet at left, Fred Leighton, N.Y.; bow, Stephen-Russell, N.Y.; drawing at upper right, Harper's Bazaar (September 1, 1940, p. 88); bracelet at right, Collection Neil Lane, L.A.

Page 130: Illustrations and jewelry, Tiffany & Co. Archives.

Page 131: Bracelet at top and brooch, Sotheby's; illustration, Tiffany & Co. Archives; necklace at center, Macklowe Gallery, N.Y.

Pages 132–33: Drawings, Tiffany & Co. Archives; brooches above left and right, Courtesy of A La Vieille Russie, Inc., N.Y.; brooch at bottom center, Tiffany & Co.; photo of Millicent Rogers, UPI/Corbis-Bettman.

Page 134: Background photo at left, UPI/Corbis-Bettman; bracelets, The Sataloff Family and the Cluchey Children.

Pages 134–35: Background photos, Corbis-Bettman; photo of rose

brooch by Kollar for Harper's Bazaar; drawings, Tiffany & Co. Archives.

Pages 136–37: "April in Paris Ball" background photo at upper left, Luis Lemus for Harper's Bazaar; necklace, Demner, N.Y./Vienna; all other photos, Ralph Morse, Life Magazine, © Time Inc.

Page 138: Emlen Etting illustration, Courtesy Stubbs Books & Prints, Inc.; brooch, Christie's, N.Y.

Page 139: Guillermo Bolin illustration, Courtesy Stubbs Books & Prints, Inc.; bracelet and earrings, Demner, N.Y./Vienna.

Page 140: Background photo, Town & Country (November 1954, p. 46); bracelet, private collection.

Page 141: Drawing, private collection; necklace, Primavera Gallery, N.Y.

Page 142: Drawings, Collection Steven Meisel; brooch at top, Fred Leighton, N.Y.; brooch at bottom and earrings, Tiffany & Co. Archives.

Page 143: Drawing, Courtesy Stubbs Books & Prints, Inc.

Pages 144–45: Background drawings, Tiffany & Co. Archives; photo at top left (collage of two photos) and photo directly below, UPI/Corbis-Bettman; photo bottom left, photographer unknown; photo at right center, from High Society: The Town & Country Picture Album (New York: Harry N. Abrams, Inc., 1996, p. 80).

Page 146: Drawing, Courtesy Stubbs Books & Prints, Inc.; bracelet, Fred Leighton, N.Y.

Page 147: Background photo by Karen Radkai, Courtesy Vogue. Copyright © 1957 (Renewed 1985) by The Condé Nast Publications Inc.; jewelry, Tiffany & Co.

Page 148: Photo by Stephen Colhoun for Town & Country (December 1956, p. 100); brooch, Tiffany & Co.

Page 149: Photo by Irving Penn, Courtesy Vogue. Copyright © 1957 (Renewed 1985) by The Condé Nast Publications Inc.; jewelry, Tiffany & Co.; compact, Sotheby's.

Pages 150–51: Drawings, private collection; jewelry, Primavera Gallery, N.Y.

Pages 152–53: Tiffany & Co. Archives.

Page 154: Drawings, Tiffany & Co. Archives; photo by Bert Stern, Courtesy Vogue. Copyright © 1963 (renewed 1991) by The Condé Nast Publications Inc.

Page 155: Drawings, Tiffany & Co. Archives; jewelry, Tiffany & Co.

Pages 156–57: Illustration, from M. Meheut, Étude de la Mer (Paris: Librairie Centrale des Beaux-Arts, © 1925); photo of brooch at left, Bert Stern, Courtesy Vogue. Copyright © 1961 (Renewed 1989) by The Condé Nast Publications Inc.; brooch at right, Tiffany & Co.

Page 158: Photo at upper left, Tibor Hirsch, Reprinted from October 6, 1962, Business Week by Special Permission © 1962 by McGraw-Hill Companies; photos inset center right and lower right, Tiffany & Co. Archives.

Page 159: Photos inset top and bottom, Bill Cunningham; 2 brooches at right and tanzanites, Tiffany & Co.

Page 161: Top photo, Courtesy House & Garden. Copyright 1968 (Renewed 1996) by The Condé Nast Publications Inc.; bottom photo, Tiffany & Co. Archives.

Page 162: Top photo, UPI/Corbis-Bettman; bottom photo, AP/Wide World Photos.

Page 163: Top photo, UPI/Corbis-Bettman; tureen, Collection Mrs. Lester Kalt; Blossfeldt photo, Courtesy Archive - Ann Und Jurgen Wilde, Köln. © 1996 Artists Rights Society (ARS), New York/VG Bild-Kunst, Bonn.

Page 164: Top photo, Courtesy Lyn Revson; bottom photo, Courtesy Henry B. Platt.

Page 165: Top photo, Erik Kvalsvik; right photo, Arthur Beck; bottom photo, Harold Krieger; photos right and bottom, © 1968, Meredith Corporation. Reprinted from *Ladies' Home Journal* with permission of photographers.

Page 166: Photo by Saul Leiter for *Harper's Bazaar* (December 1966, p. 155).

Page 167: Drawings, Courtesy Stubbs Books & Prints, Inc.; frog and dragon brooches, Tiffany & Co. Archives; walrus and disc brooches, private collection; ram's head brooch, Fred Leighton, N.Y.

Page 168: Photo by Penati, Courtesy *Vogue.* Copyright © 1970 by The Condé Nast Publications Inc.; photo of necklace, Tiffany & Co. Archives.

Page 169: Photo, UPI/Corbis-Bettman.

Page 170: Photo at center, © Hiro; photo at bottom, Josh Haskin.

Page 171: Photo at center, © Bill King/Bill King Photographs, Inc.; bracelet, private collection.

Page 172: Photo of model by Bert Stern, Courtesy *Vogue.* Copyright © 1963 (Renewed 1991) by The Condé Nast Publications Inc.; jewelry, Tiffany & Co.; drawings, Tiffany & Co. Archives.

Page 173: Photo of model by Henry Clarke, Courtesy *Vogue.* Copyright © 1962 (Renewed 1990) by The Condé Nast Publications Inc.; drawing, Tiffany & Co. Archives.

Page 174: Photo © Hiro.

Page 175: Photo by Helmut Newton, Courtesy *Vogue.* Copyright © 1964 (Renewed 1992) by The Condé Nast Publications Inc.; necklace, Tiffany & Co.

Page 176: Background, Tiffany & Co. Archives; jewelry, private collection.

Page 177: Brooch, Sotheby's.

Pages 178–79: Backgrounds, Tiffany & Co. Archives; jewelry, Tiffany & Co.

Page 180 (photos, clockwise from upper left): © Bill King/Bill King Photographs Inc.; Gene Laurents, Courtesy *Vogue.* Copyright © 1969 (Renewed 1997) by The Condé Nast Publications Inc.; James Moore for *Harper's Bazaar;* Jerry Salvati for *Town & Country.*

Page 181: Photo © 1965 Richard Avedon, All Rights Reserved.

Page 182: Left photo, Penati; center photo, Gene Laurents; photos Courtesy *Vogue.* Copyright © 1968 (Renewed 1968) by The Condé Nast Publications Inc.

Page 183: Photos, Sotheby's.

Page 184: Photo, Neal Barr.

Page 185: Jewelry, Tiffany & Co.

Page 186: Photo, Marion Curtis/DMI.

Page 187: Left photo, *New York Daily News;* right photo, Ruven Afanador/Outline Press.

Page 188: Top photo, Fifth Avenue Display Photographers; bottom photos, © Jim Henson Productions, Inc.

Page 189: Photo, Philip-Lorca diCorcia.

Page 190: Photo, Nick Malan Studio International.

Page 191: Photo, Rodger-Max Barrow.

Page 192: Photo, Nick Malan Studio International.

Page 193: Photo, Fifth Avenue Display Photographers.

Page 194: Left photo, Carlton Davis; right photo, Craig Cutler.

Page 195: Drawing, Joe Eula; jewelry, Tiffany & Co.

Page 196: Photo, Tiffany & Co. Archives.

Page 197: Top photo, Walter Chin; photos bottom right and left, Copyright © 1980 The Estate of Robert Mapplethorpe.

Page 198: Top photos, Craig Cutler; bottom photo, Marina Schiano.

Page 199: Photo, Hiro, © Kuma Enterprise.

Page 200: Photo of leaf necklace, Tiffany & Co. Archives.

Page 201 (photos, from top): Richard Gillard/Royal Focus - Picture Library; Andrew Murray/Sygma; Corbis-Bettman; Bill Cunningham/*W*; photo of brooch, Tiffany & Co. Archives.

Page 202: Photo, © Bill King/Bill King Photographs, Inc.

Pages 203–7: Photos, Hiro, © Kuma Enterprise.

Pages 208–14: Photos, Skrebneski.

Page 215: Photo, © Bill King/Bill King Photographs, Inc.

Page 216: Photo, Kenro Izu.

Pages 217–18: Photos, Skrebneski.

Page 219: Top photo, Eric Boman; bottom photo, Raoul Manuel Schnell/*Madame Magazine.*

Pages 220–21: Photo, Doug Rosa; upper right, Tiffany & Co.

Pages 222–23: Photos, Manfredi Bellati.

Page 224: Jewelry, Tiffany & Co.; background photo, Courtesy *House & Garden.* Copyright © 1968 (renewed 1996) by The Condé Nast Publications Inc.

Page 225: Jewelry, Tiffany & Co.; drawing at top, private collection; drawing at bottom, from M. Meheut, *Étude de la Mer* (Paris: Librairie Centrale des Beaux-Arts, © 1925).

Page 226: Top photo, Martin Mistretta; bottom photo, Mikael Jansson.

Page 227: Photo, Carlton Davis; photo inset at top, Craig Cutler.

Pages 228–29: Left photo, Carlton Davis; right, background photo, Tiffany & Co. Archives.

Pages 230–31: Photos, Rita Maas.

Page 232: Photo, Bob Frame.

Page 233: Photo, Craig Cutler.

Page 234: Top photo, Mikael Jansson; bottom photo, Craig Cutler.

Page 235: Photo, Kenro Izu.

Page 240: Background photo by Bruehl-Bourges, Courtesy *Vogue.* Copyright 1933 (renewed 1961) by The Condé Nast Publications Inc.; jewelry in foreground, from left, Fred Leighton, N.Y.; Firestone and Parson, Boston; Stephen-Russell, N.Y.; Fred Leighton, N.Y.

Acknowledgments

The author and Tiffany & Co. would like to thank William R. Chaney, chairman of Tiffany's, and Michael Kowalski, president of Tiffany's, for their encouragement and support; Tiffany's Eric Erickson for his many exceptional contributions to the aesthetics of this book as well as for his diplomacy and genius at negotiating the minefields of reproduction rights to the photographic images; Billy Cunningham and his associate Martin Friedman for so much of the book's magnificent and innovative photography; Rollins Maxwell for his uniquely insightful research as well as for his work on captions and credits; Annamarie Sandecki, Tiffany's archivist, for her orchestration of Tiffany & Co. archival materials; Louisa Bann and Ruth Caccavale, Tiffany's assistant archivists, for finding the unfindable in our archives; MaryAnn Aurora for her genius as traffic controller and coordinator for all materials; Margaret Rennolds Chace, our editor, for all her vision, insights, and enthusiasm; Carol Ann Robson, our designer at Abrams, for all the great originality and visual excitement she brought to the book; Condé Nast Publications Inc. and Hearst Publications Inc. for their extraordinary generosity in offering the use of photographs from their matchless archives; Christie's and Sotheby's for the use of their photograph archives; Alastair Duncan for his help with Louis Comfort Tiffany materials; Ralph Esmerian for his vital support; Richard Horst and Horst P. Horst for their great generosity and assistance with imagery; Hiro for the contribution of his splendid and celebrated photography of the works of Elsa Peretti; Victor Skrebneski for allowing us to include his incomparable jewelry photography; Jane Stubbs for her expertise and help in the world of fashion illustration; Dr. Joseph and Ruth Sataloff for having the vision to have preserved a significant portion of Tiffany's twentieth-century jewelry design history; Maurice Galli, Tiffany's senior jewelry designer, for his superbly rendered illustrations; and last but far from least, Tiffany's publicist, Eleanor Lambert Berkson, for formulating the original concept and for giving *Tiffany's 20th Century* its title.

John Loring

An early color photographic illustration by Bruehl-Bourges from *Vogue*'s December 1, 1933, issue shows a collection of Tiffany's flexible diamond, colored precious stone, and platinum jewels. Four similar Tiffany's flexible bracelets from the 1930s are overlaid on the original image.

J is for jewels